Praise for *13 Powerful Ways to Pray*

"Whether you have a mature and robust prayer life or are just discovering the joy of personal prayer for the first time, *13 Powerful Ways to Pray* will be a true gift for your spiritual life. Father Tobin offers encouragement, instruction, and practical wisdom to help draw you into a deeper relationship with Jesus Christ and the world around you. Especially helpful are insights on praying through periods of pain, conflict, spiritual dryness, and even simply the busyness of day-to-day life."

—Lisa M. Hendey

Founder of CatholicMom.com and author of *The Grace of Yes*

"Three words describe this book best—it is practical, practical, and practical!"

—Bert Ghezzi

Author of *The Power of Daily Prayer*

"An amazingly thorough and balanced book for every Christian. Anyone, whether a beginner or an established pray-er, can benefit from Fr. Eamon Tobin's perspective on prayer. I believe that this book will speak to the hearts of all who are seeking God, who is actually seeking us!"

—Monsignor David L. Toups, STD

Rector of St. Vincent de Paul Regional Seminary,
Boynton Beach, Florida

· 13 ·
Powerful
— WAYS TO —
PRAY

EAMON TOBIN

BEACON PUBLISHING
North Palm Beach, Florida

ISBN: 978-1-942611-88-2 (softcover)

Design byMadeline Harris
Interior byRachel Lee

Imprimi Potest
William A. Nugent, C.SS.R.
Provincial, St. Louis Province, The Redemptorists
Imprimatur
Monsignor Maurice F. Byrne
Vice Chancellor, Archdiocese of St. Louis

Scripture texts used are taken from the *New American Bible with the Revised
New Testament* copyright © 1986 by the Confraternity of Christian Doctrine,
Washington, DC, and are used with permission. All rights reserved.

Library of Congress Cataloging-in-Publication Data
Names: Tobin, Eamon, author.
Title: 13 powerful ways to pray / Father Eamon Tobin.
Other titles: Thirteen powerful ways to pray
Description: North Palm Beach, FL : Beacon, 2016. | Originally published:
Liguori, Mo. : Liguori Publications, c1989. | Includes bibliographical references.
Identifiers: LCCN 2016018825 (print) | LCCN 2016019088 (ebook) | ISBN
9781942611882 (pbk.) | ISBN 9781942611899 (ebk.)
Subjects: LCSH: Prayer—Catholic Church.
Classification: LCC BV210.3 .T63 2016 (print) | LCC BV210.3 (ebook) | DDC
248.3/2—dc23
LC record available at https://lccn.loc.gov/2016018825

Dynamic Catholic® and Be Bold. Be Catholic.® and The Best Version of
Yourself® are registered trademarks of The Dynamic Catholic Institute.

For more information on this title or other books and CDs available through
the Dynamic Catholic Book Program, please visit www.DynamicCatholic.com.

The Dynamic Catholic Institute
5081 Olympic Blvd • Erlanger • Kentucky • 41018
Phone: 1–859–980–7900
Email: info@DynamicCatholic.com

Fourth printing, November 2017

Printed in the United States of America

DEDICATION

To the wonderful parishioners of
Ascension Catholic Church Family

Contents

Preface

Remembering that I come from a race of people who for hundreds of years have been praying in the Christian way comforts, challenges, and sustains me in my efforts to be a praying person. Reflecting on the fact that my people have been a praying people for so many generations motivates me to keep alive such a wonderful praying tradition and to add to it in some small way.

I am also comforted, challenged, and sustained by the fact that I come from a family for whom prayer was an essential part of life. With affection I remember seeing my father kneeling on the kitchen floor while saying his "morning prayers" before going out to the fields to work all day. I remember my stepmother and my Aunt Daisy making their daily Holy Hour in the midmorning as they went about their morning chores. At midday everyone prayed the Angelus. It was especially edifying to see the big, strong men out in the fields stop their work, take off their caps, and silently pray,

"The angel of the Lord declared unto Mary . . ." After supper in the evening, the whole family (and anyone else who happened to be there) got down on their knees and prayed the Rosary. All of my aunts and uncles were people of prayer. Growing up in such an atmosphere reinforced in me, time and time again, the importance of prayer.

My grade school teacher was a very wonderful and prayerful lady. Consequently, prayer was an important part of my formation during my elementary school years. The high school I attended as a boarder was run by diocesan priests. Daily Mass, morning and evening prayers, and visits to the Blessed Sacrament were integral parts of each day. Each year we also had two retreats.

My seven years in the seminary were in a very special way a time of formation in the varied ways of Christian prayer. Besides the spiritual exercises that were an essential part of daily life, each seminarian had a spiritual director with whom he could chat on a regular basis about his spiritual life.

Since my ordination to the priesthood in 1972, I have tried, with reasonable success, to remain faithful to an hour of *personal* prayer each day. In my parish work I have also had the opportunity to pray with diverse groups of Protestants and Catholics from whom I have learned much about the art of praying. I share these thoughts in order that you may know something of the background that I bring to this topic. In no way do I consider myself an expert in prayer. I am still very much a beginner and a learner. When it comes to prayer, all persons are perpetual students. Jesus alone is the Master, Teacher, and Expert.

Personally I find prayer to be both a consoling and difficult experience. It is consoling and enjoyable when I believe I am making contact with God whether on a feeling or faith level, when I discover new insights into his ways, when I receive answers to my petitions, and when I simply experience his loving presence and mercy. Praying is difficult for me when I am distracted or unfocused, when my prayer is dry, when I think my efforts to pray are going nowhere, and when I think I have lost contact with God.

I experience all of the common problems that people experience in prayer. I wonder how I should pray. I am often plagued by distractions in prayer. Sometimes I wonder if the time I spend in formal prayer could not be used more effectively. This question, coupled with a busy schedule, sometimes cause me to cut short my prayer time. I find it difficult to integrate prayer and life and see them as one act of worship before God. Sometimes I find prayer to be downright dull and boring, and I wonder how God could be interested or pleased by my feeble attempts to pray.

Despite all these difficulties I still find prayer to be absolutely essential to my life. Prayer is to my spirit what food is to my body. It is the bread of my spiritual life. To quit or neglect prayer is to quit or neglect to care for the core of my being (my spirit) and its deepest desire (intimacy with my Creator). Without prayer I would be a person without the wine of life (see John 2:3), a noisy gong and a clanging cymbal (see 1 Corinthians 13:1). Many, many years ago St. Augustine said that all persons were created for communion with God and that their hearts would never rest until they rested in God. It is my strong belief in these words of Augustine that causes me to persevere in prayer and to say no (at least most of the time) to all of the things that compete with prayer for my time. I also try to remain faithful to prayer because, as a minister of the Lord, I deeply believe that without him I cannot be fruitful. In the Gospel of John, Jesus says:

> I am the vine, you are the branches. Whoever remains in me and I in him, will bear much fruit, because without me you can do nothing. (John 15:5)

Ministry not rooted in Jesus the Vine may have all the signs of success, but in reality it will be only "sound and fury signifying nothing" (Shakespeare). Ministry rooted in Christ *may seem* in the eyes of the world to be a failure, but in the eyes of Jesus, it will be most fruitful. For those who are raised in a work-ethic, do-it-yourself society, it is not easy to believe that hours spent in quiet prayer can bring people closer to the kingdom than their own best laid plans and efforts. For me "wasting time" in prayer expresses my belief that it is God who is the Creator and Transformer of life, who makes the flowers grow and yields a rich harvest. When I begin to substitute work for prayer, I know I am believing the lie that proclaims, "If I work hard enough, things will really happen." This may be true in the secular realm, but it is certainly not true in the spiritual realm. In the latter "things happen" when I generously cooperate with God's movement of grace at work in me and outside of me.

Despite the vast number of books available on prayer, I have decided to write another book because I believe each person, as a unique expression of God, can discover something unique about God and how to relate to him. Just as no two sunrises or smiles are exactly the same, no two persons approach prayer in exactly the same way. Therefore, when people speak or write about prayer—when they tell how they relate to God and how God works in them—a new and unique image of prayer comes into being. Speaking more pragmatically, I decided to write this book on prayer because I wanted to gather together what I consider to be some keys to effective prayer (Part One) and some important traditional and contemporary forms of prayer (Part Two).

Finally, this book is intended to be very practical. It is very much a how-to approach to prayer. For example, in Part One I not only speak about some keys to effective prayer, I also offer practical suggestions on how to integrate such keys or basics into one's daily prayer life. In Part Two I not only explain several different prayer forms, I also offer several examples of how to use them. At the end of each key and each chapter, I include some Questions for Personal Reflection and Small-Group Discussion and a Suggested Prayer Exercise.

What Is Prayer?

He [Jesus] was praying in a certain place, and when he had finished, one of his disciples said to him, "Lord, teach us to pray just as John taught his disciples." He said to them, "When you pray, say: Father, hallowed be your name, your kingdom come. Give us each day our daily bread and forgive us our sins for we ourselves forgive everyone in debt to us, and do not subject us to the final test."

Luke 11:1–4

People often ask: "What is prayer?" The answer to that question is not easy because there is no one definition of prayer that is exhaustive. Most definitions have some element of truth to them, but none of them says it all. Because of this limitation, one definition may be more accurate and helpful to some people, while another definition may be more accurate and helpful to others. It is useful to share different ideas on the meaning of prayer because such sharing can help us to clarify what it is we think we are doing when we pray. It can also help us to become aware of definitions that are not very accurate or helpful. We can only grow or go forward if we are aware of where we are presently standing.

Here are two traditional definitions of prayer that are sometimes criticized today. The first is this: "Prayer is the raising up of the mind and heart to God." Some spiritual writers criticize this definition because it seems to imply that the primary initiative in prayer is ours and not God's, that we decide to pray. It would be more accurate to say, "Prayer is our *response* to God's touch in our lives." We pray or call out to God because *he has moved us* to pray and not because we think it is a good idea to make contact with God. The initiative is always with God. In him we live, move, and have our being. We call out to God only because he has first called out to us. We find God only because he has been looking for us (see Genesis 3:8–9). A key truth to remember in the spiritual realm is that *all is gift*. We move toward God only because he is inviting us to come and enabling us to move in his direction (see Luke 10:21).

A second, frequently used definition of prayer describes it as "talking to God." Again the danger here is that we may think that in prayer the initiative is with us and not God. We need to keep in mind that if we talk to God, it is only because he has moved us to talk to him. A second danger in using the "talking to God" description of prayer is that we may think that prayer is basically a monologue wherein we do all the talking and God does all the listening. Central to growth in prayer is learning to listen to what God is saying and where he is guiding us.

Citing St. Thérèse of Lisieux, *The Catechism of the Catholic Church* states that "prayer is a surge of the heart, it is a simple look turned toward heaven, it is a cry of recognition and of love embracing both trial and joy" (*CCC*, 2558). Prayer can also be defined as "opening to God." In true prayer we expose ourselves to God as sunbathers expose themselves to the sun. Prayer is allowing God to love us; it is our becoming aware of God's great love for us. We become present and responsive to a God who is all around us and in whom we live, move, and have our being. Prayer is not an attempt to contact a missing, hard-to-find God. Rather it is our graced effort to be open, attentive, and responsive to a God whose presence fills the universe and who frequently becomes present to us in tangible ways.

In the journey to Emmaus, we witness two disciples walking with Jesus (see Luke 24:13–35). At first they do not recognize him as Jesus. Only later did they really recognize who it was who had walked with them. In the same way, many of us may experience God, but we may not recognize the fact. Often only after a particular encounter or event do we recognize that God was present and active in our midst. Thus a big part of prayer is learning to be sensitive to the "in-breakings" of God into the journey of life. To describe prayer as opening to God is particularly helpful when we find prayer difficult because the emphasis is not on *our* making things happen, but rather on our being *open* to what *God* might make happen.

Prayer can also be defined as "the experience of connecting with God." There are some people we have known by sight for years, having seen them at church or at work, but we have never actually encountered them. Then one day we meet and talk. The potential for meeting or connecting was always there, but it has not happened until now. It is somewhat the same with God and prayer.

God is there—that is, within us and all around us—and we are there, but we just don't connect. A real "moment of prayer" happens when we are gifted with the grace of connecting with God.

Prayer can also be described as "waiting upon the Lord." Day after day we go to prayer and wait. Sometimes we come away and we are still waiting, hoping, and expecting. But sometimes he comes and fills us with his light, giving us a tiny glimpse of who he is, and then he is gone. Then the waiting begins once again.

Prayer is *longing* for greater union with God. "As the hind longs for the running waters, so my soul longs for you, O God" (Psalm 42:2).

Prayer is *glimpsing* the beauty of God, just as we get a glimmer of the sun now and again on a cloudy day.

Prayer is *standing before* God in radical poverty, without illusions, before the infinite richness of God.

Prayer is *discovering* all that God has already given us and growing in our appreciation of his gifts.

Finally, prayer can be defined as "a personal relationship with God." Just as communication, properly used, is a tool that enables us to develop a close relationship with other human persons, so prayer is a tool that will make it more possible for us to develop a loving relationship with God. Consider the parallels. Generally speaking, our ability to relate to God will be no better than our ability to relate to other human beings.

In fact, we can say that our style of relating on a human level will usually manifest itself in our prayer. For example:

- If we have a tendency to dominate human conversations, we will more than likely do most of the talking in prayer.

- If on the human level we usually wear our hearts on our sleeves, we will probably find it easy to reveal our true selves to the Lord.

- If we rarely give ourselves permission to express our tough feelings—anger, jealousy, inadequacy, and the like—we will probably not talk to God about such feelings. On the contrary, if we have become accustomed to "flying off the handle" with others, we will most likely not have a problem getting angry with God.

- If we find it hard to give and receive forgiveness on the human level, we may also find it hard to accept God's mercy and to "forgive God" when he isn't moving in the way we think he should.

- If we are inclined to be utilitarian, manipulative, and controlling in our human relationships, we may consciously (but more likely unconsciously) bring the same attitudes into our relationship with God.

The way we are with people is the way we are with God. There is a danger that we fool ourselves into thinking that we are different with God than we are with people. Because we bring our style of communicating with others into our prayer, it is very important for us to be aware of our pluses and minuses in human communication.

Each of us is born with a potential to relate, a potential that must be developed if we are going to communicate effectively with other people. At this point in our lives, that potential to relate has been developed to a lesser or greater extent. If presently our human potential to relate isn't very good, that will diminish our potential to relate to God through prayer. For example, if we have very little ability to put aside our own concerns and preoccupations in order to be truly present to another, without a miracle of grace we are going to find it very difficult to hear the voice of God. Or if, on the human level, we have developed very little ability to trust others, we may find it hard to trust God. So each of us brings to prayer particular relational strengths and limitations that will probably either help or hinder our relationship with God.

Generally speaking, we can say that as we grow in our ability to relate on a human level, we will be preparing good soil for our relationship with God. Married couples who participate in a Marriage Encounter weekend often report that their newfound ability to relate to each other also enhances their relationship with God. For example, just as the weekend helps them relate to each other more on a heart (sharing of feelings) than head (sharing of thoughts) level, so the weekend helps them relate to God on a heart or feeling level. It is through our human relationships that we develop the skills necessary to better our relationship with God.

While there are many parallels between human and divine-human communication, there are a couple of differences. An obvious one is that we cannot see God, hear his voice, or hold his hand. We have to depend on the gift of faith to believe that God is present to us and that he does indeed speak to us. A much more important difference is that in the divine-human relationship God is *always* faithful, loving, and merciful. God also has the power to bring about on a divine-human level something that seems unlikely or impossible on a human level. For example, even though we have never really trusted someone on a human level, it is possible that God could bypass our human limitation or heal it, thus enabling us to trust him. So while God usually works through our human gifts and talents, we must never limit God's work in our lives to such gifts and talents.

This Introduction has examined several definitions of prayer—none of which completely defines it because prayer remains a mystery. We have also seen that the meaning of prayer will change as our relationship with God develops. With this background we can now proceed to examine the four keys to an effective prayer life and explain the various types of prayer.

Questions for Personal Reflection and Small-Group Discussion

1. What spoke to you most in this chapter?
2. What insight in these pages made the greatest impression on you?
3. Which of the above attempts to define prayer appealed to you the most? How would you define prayer?
4. Can you see how we tend to bring our human way of relating into our prayer? Give some examples from your own life.
5. What was your experience with the suggested prayer exercise offered below?

Suggested Prayer Exercise

The next time you spend time in prayer, be attentive to which definition of prayer in this chapter best describes your approach to prayer. Also, be open to a form of prayer that would fit into one of the other descriptions of prayer—e.g., prayer as being *open* to God.

PART ONE

FOUR KEYS TO AN EFFECTIVE PRAYER LIFE

When it comes to our relationship with God, there are at least four essential keys to an effective relationship with our triune God. Even though each of us prays in a different way, all of us should attend to these four basics in prayer:

1) Developing a positive image of God and self;
2) Being honest with God;
3) Connecting prayer with daily life;
4) Listening to God in prayer.

If we ignore or are inattentive to any of these four essentials or keys, our relationship with God will be defective in some way.

Before examining each of these keys, it is important to understand the meaning of the words *effective* and *keys* when used in connection with prayer.

Effective Prayer: On the human level our attempts to communicate with each other can be effective or ineffective. They may be ineffective because deep down (perhaps unconsciously) either one or both of the parties may not want to communicate. Sometimes the problem is that, despite the presence of good will, very little intimacy is experienced because of a lack of basic communication skills. Some people have poorly developed listening skills; others are unable to confront in a mature way and reconcile differences in a reasonable way. On the other hand, when two people want very much to communicate with each other and have developed some basic communication skills, there is every chance that they will experience a good degree of understanding, trust, acceptance, and intimacy.

Now, just as there is effective and ineffective human communication, there is effective and ineffective divine-human communication. Some people, for example, pray (or rather "say prayers") all their lives and still do not make contact with God. Their prayer does not seem to affect their lives or the way they communicate with other people. They are often harsh and critical of self and others, have little or no social conscience, and are fearful and anxious about the future. Obviously the prayer or communication of such people is ineffective and leaves much to be desired both with God and with others.

In contrast to such faulty communication, effective prayer, of its very nature, facilitates human and spiritual growth and enhances our relationships with others and with God. It leads to growth in faith, hope, and love of God, others, and self. Effective or real prayer helps us to face evil courageously and place our trust in God when we walk in the valley of darkness (see Psalm 23). Effective prayer opens us to the experience of God's unconditional love and the acceptance of his incomprehensible ways. It gradually helps us to be attentive and responsive to the needs of others, especially the poor. Finally, effective prayer should help us accept and integrate the different dimensions and strivings of our being.

If these growth patterns are not developing in our lives, then maybe we should reevaluate our way of praying. Of course, the benefits of effective prayer will not happen overnight. In fact, there will be periods of time when we wonder if anything positive is happening in our prayer life. But over the long haul, we can expect to grow closer to God and others if our prayer is honest and genuine.

Keys to Effective Prayer: The word *keys* does not imply that if we do certain things (press certain keys), we will *automatically* experience intimacy with God. Such belief would be seriously mistaken and blind us to the fact that, *in the spiritual life, all is gift* and union with God cannot be earned. The use of the word *keys* refers to some basic truths that we need to pay attention to so that we become receptive soil for God's transforming work in us. The phrase *receptive soil* reminds us that prayer and its goal, our transformation in Christ (see Galatians 4:19), are pure gift. All we can do is pray for this gift and do what we can to create the conditions that will make us good soil for God's transforming work. William Shannon, in *Seeking the Face of God*, writes: "It is true to say we don't pray, but rather *we let it happen in us.* The best we can do is to prepare and dispose ourselves to let it happen." The following four chapters will examine the four keys needed to help us prepare for an effective relationship with God.

Developing a Positive Image of God and Self

*God sent his only Son into the world so that we
might have life through him. In this is love: not
that we have loved God, but that he loved us
and sent his Son as expiation for our sins.*

1 John 4:9–10

*If we really know ourselves to be loved by God, sooner
or later our spontaneous response will be to love
God in return. . . . The more rooted we are in love,
the more generously shall we live our faith and put
it into practice. . . . The knowledge that God loves
us enables us to love ourselves without excuse and
without questioning. We love ourselves as we are
because our faith has convinced us that God does so.*

Peter G. van Breemen, SJ

Few factors have the potential to affect the quality of our prayer life as much as our image of God and self. On a human level, the image and feelings we have for another person and how we perceive the other person to feel about us will usually have a tremendous effect on how we relate to that person. For example, we will approach and relate to a person whom we love and whom we perceive loves us in a different way than we will to a person for whom we have little or no feeling and whom we think does not particularly care for us. Our own self-image also will affect the way we approach and relate to people. If we have a positive image of ourselves, we will go out to people and relate to them with confidence, assuming they will like us. If we think we are not very lovable, we will approach people with self-doubt, fearful that they may reject us and not find us lovable. And if we believe that people will only accept us when we behave in certain ways, we will be inclined to be unreal with them, behaving only in ways we perceive to be acceptable to them.

How is all this connected to our relationship with God and our efforts at prayer? Well, God is a person, and prayer is our attempt to relate with a personal God. We have already shown how the same basic dynamics are at work in our relationship with God as are at work in our relationships with other people. What helps or hinders us in our attempts to relate to other people will also help or hinder us in our relationship with God.

It is very important that we spend some quality time reflecting on these questions and perhaps sharing our reflections with a spiritual guide. We need to check the images of God and self from which we operate and become aware of some of the consequences of these images. For example, if we perceive God to be a policeman-type person who imposes numerous rules and demands strict adherence to them, our relationship with him will be characterized by fear, distance, and perhaps resentment. If we are overly scrupulous, we will believe consciously—or more likely unconsciously—that God is a tyrant who is impossible to please and who is ready to pounce on us for our failures. If we experience God as withholding himself from us, we will be reluctant to petition him for our needs. If we experience him as a loving Father, we will approach him with trust, relaxation, and love. If we experience God as merciful, we will not hesitate to talk to him about our failures, knowing that his love for us is not based on our good performance.

While we may at times *say* we believe in a God of love and mercy, our harsh, judgmental attitudes toward our own failures and those of others tell a different story. Sometimes there is quite a difference between the images of God that we *think* we have and the images of God that *actually* influence our lives. Most, if not all, of us carry around some primitive, destructive images of God that can particularly affect us in times of stress.

Once, while listening to a retreat leader speak about primitive images of God, I became aware that one of my primitive images is that God is a *demanding* person who is only pleased with me when I am being good and obeying his commandments. So while I may believe on an intellectual level in a God of unconditional love, I may function on an operational level with an image of God who loves me only when I am keeping the rules.

Our image of God often derives from childhood relationships with parents or authority figures. As I reflect on my relationship with my father, I become aware that I perceive him to be a good man, but also a demanding man. Seemingly I project the same demanding image onto God, and so I perceive God as difficult to please, loving me only when I am obeying the commandments.

The Scriptures give us several different and interesting images of God. God is described as the shepherd caring for his sheep (see Psalm 23); as the grocer providing food for the people (see Numbers 11:31); as a mother cherishing her offspring (see Isaiah 49:15) or weeping over her rebellious children (see Matthew 23:37–39); as teacher (see Matthew 5—7); as healer of the sick and friend of sinners (see Luke 15); as one denouncing the righteous (see Matthew 23:13–32) and the corrupt (see Matthew 21:12-17); as challenger of the rich (see Matthew 19:16–26); and as one who demands all from a potential disciple (see Luke 9:23–26,57–62). Of course, no individual image or set of images can comprehend the Incomprehensible God. St. Thomas Aquinas tells us: "If you can comprehend God, he is not God, for God is ultimately a Mystery." Nevertheless, it is legitimate for us humans, particularly at the early stages of our spiritual lives, to make use of human images to help us in our relationship with God.

IMAGING GOD AS LOVE

Of all the images of God that can serve us well in our relationship with him, the image of God as unconditional lover is the most important. Insofar as we have not experienced God as love in the *deepest center* of our being (as opposed to acquired knowledge in the head), to that extent we have not experienced the Good News. It has been well said that the Good News is that God loves us, no strings attached; the sad news is that the vast majority of us do not believe the Good News with our heart.

God must sometimes get very frustrated with us as we ignore his efforts to convince us of his unconditional love. The primary reason he sent Jesus into the world was to reveal to us in a human way the extent of his love. When Jesus was dying on the cross—with arms outstretched and blood pouring from his crucified body and heart—it was as if the Father was saying to every individual who was ever born: "This is how much I love you. My words are not empty; they are written with the blood of my own Son." The Scriptures tell us that Jesus died for us while we were still in our sins. St. Paul writes:

> Indeed, only with difficulty does one die for a just person, though perhaps for a good person one might even find courage to die. But God proves his love for us in that while we were still sinners Christ died for us. (Romans 5:7–8)

Pope Francis also emphasizes the importance of us having a sense of God's love when we pray when he says: "At the heart of prayer is the love of God, the source of our life, who constantly 'caresses' us with his own love."

When we doubt the truth of God's love, it is as if the power of original sin (expressed in a statement like "I wonder if I am really lovable") grabs hold of us. When such darkness invades our minds and hearts, we can reject it by renewing our baptismal promises in words like these: "Satan, I reject the lies you are now placing in my heart about my basic goodness. I believe that Jesus loves me with all my flaws and failures. Jesus, I believe this. Help me to dispel my unbelief."

Of course, the main reason we doubt that God loves us unconditionally is that we may never have experienced unconditional love on a human level. Most of the time we experience love only when our behavior is acceptable to others: We try to be good so that others will love us. Consciously or unconsciously we think it is the same with God. While we may say that God's love for us is not determined by our actions, our *behavior* often says that we actually believe that God loves us only when we keep his commandments. We try to be virtuous so that God will love us. In *The Christian Vision: The Truth That Sets Us Free*, Jesuit priest John Powell writes that God's response to this human thinking would be:

> "O child of my heart, you've got it backwards. You shouldn't think that if you become more virtuous I will love you more, because already you have all my love as a

free gift. You don't have to change so that I will love you more. What you really need to know is how much I have always loved you. Oh, then . . . you will really change."

Sometimes we see the truth of these beautiful words when persons fall in love and make dramatic changes in their lives. The experience of feeling loved by others motivates them to *want* to make changes in their lives and *want* to respond with love. Love effects a change that no law and no amount of force could bring about.

In the Christian journey our primary aim is not to be good so that God will love us, but rather to be open to experiencing God's transforming love, which in turn will motivate us, more than anything else, to *want* to be Christlike in thought, word, and deed (see 2 Corinthians 5:14–21). This also reminds us to use some of our prayer time to be still before the loving presence of God so he can communicate to us that we are loved by him regardless of our performance.

Unfortunately, most of us tend to be so busy or active in prayer that we fail to give God a chance to reveal his love to us. Yet this standing or sitting still before God is crucial for our spiritual growth. It is especially important to sit still before God when we are aware of specific sins that we have just committed. It is a healing grace for us to be able to face God with our sins and know that he still loves us. As we know, Jesus died for us *while we were still in our sin* (see Romans 5:8). Christians are "loved sinners." Knowing this, not just in our heads but in our hearts, is indeed a tremendous grace.

Are there any practical suggestions that will help us to experience God's unconditional love? Yes, there are. Here are some worthwhile ones. First, we can pray for the gift of knowing in our hearts that God loves us. We can say: "Jesus, lead me more deeply into the unconditional love that our Father has for me." Second, we can try to recognize and name the particular ways that we believe God is presently loving us. Sometimes children don't recognize the many ways their parents love them. Likewise, we are often blind to the many ways that God loves us. We need to work at becoming conscious of the simple ways in which God loves us in the flow of a day. A third suggestion is to try to develop a grateful attitude toward life, realizing that all the good and the apparently not good happenings in life come from the loving hand of God. Fourth, we should try to see an expression of God's love in the genuine expressions of love that people give us. The experience of intimacy with another readies our hearts to experience intimacy with God our Father.

Coming to prayer with a heartfelt (and not just head-wise) sense of God's compassionate love for us should help to make prayer much more relaxing. In the presence of a loving Father, we don't have to prove anything, dress up nicely, or be formal. We are loved just as we are. Our loving Father says to us: "Come as you are; be yourself; enjoy your time with me. If you want to talk and pour out your heart about something, that's okay. If you want to rest in my presence, snuggle up in my lap and arms, that's okay, too."

IMAGING OURSELVES AS LOVABLE

We need to remember that a key factor in an effective prayer life is experiencing ourselves as lovable. A poor self-image can play havoc with our relationships on both a human and spiritual level. When we suffer from a poor opinion of ourselves, we are inclined to assume that God (and other people) share this opinion. If we don't see much to love in ourselves, we will find it difficult to believe that God sees much to love in us. Such a belief will keep us at a distance from God. In effect, to question or deny our own goodness is like questioning or denying that we were created "very good," as we are told in Genesis 1:31. Perhaps we should sometimes tell our Creator that we are sorry for the times we felt that he must have had an "off day" when he created us.

What can we do to come to a greater sense of our innate goodness and beauty? How can we begin to see ourselves as God sees us? The following are a few suggestions.

First suggestion: We can use the Word of God to transform and shape the way we see ourselves. Ultimately, *our self-image is formed by the loving Word of God or deformed by the destructive words of others.* Our self-image is shaped by the words we believe about ourselves. Which words are we listening to and believing—the affirming Word of God or the destructive words of others?

The only reason we end up with a poor self-image is because we allowed destructive words to enter and shape the core of our being. For example, some of us may believe we are stupid or no good. This happens because, at some point in our formation, someone said to us, "You are stupid and no good," and unfortunately we believed that person. The words, "I am stupid and no good," became part of how we saw ourselves. But—and this is a crucial point—the only reason why such words became a destructive force in our lives is because we dwelt on them, pondered them, and reflected on them so much that they reached not just our ears but the very core of our being where our self-concept is formed or deformed.

To counteract this, we must learn to dwell on, ponder, and reflect on the loving words of God and others. We do this when we allow the affirmation of God and others to touch not just our skin, as it were, but the very core of our being. But we allow the loving words of God and others to touch just our skin when we do not receive those words into our being and believe them. For example, we may receive an affirming letter from someone, quickly read it, toss it aside, and forget about the loving words written there. On the other hand, if we receive a negative letter, we may not only read it, but keep pondering it all day and perhaps for several days. How sad that so many of us tend to toss aside so easily the affirming words we receive while we tend to hold onto the negative, destructive words.

To help us as we listen to God's Word and allow it to affirm us in our self-worth, we will do well to consider the words of John's Gospel: "As the Father loves me, so I also love you" (John 15:9).

We begin by using our imagination to *visualize* Jesus

speaking these words to us. We can imagine Jesus sitting on a chair across from us. He is looking at us with love and saying, "As my Father loves me, so do I love you."

Then we should try to allow those words to enter our being—to touch not just our ears but also our hearts. Perhaps we may wish to repeat the words of Jesus over and over again, giving them time to touch and shape the core of our being. We should recall everything that has been said about the importance of dwelling on the words spoken to us. Those words cannot bear fruit unless we reflect on them over and over again. Here we should imitate Mary who pondered the words that were spoken to her (see Luke 2:19).

Then we should *verbalize* our acceptance of the affirmation and love that Jesus offers. We can say, "Yes, Jesus, I believe you love me. Help me to believe it more deeply." So often we deny or fail to accept gracefully the affirmation offered to us by God and others. When the experience of affirmation and love is truly received and pondered, it has the power "to make us over again."

Then, having received, pondered, and accepted the word of affirmation, the next thing we need to do is thank God for his loving words. The act of giving thanks is a concrete sign that we have accepted God's word of affirmation. We could give thanks to God in simple words like this: "I thank you, Lord, for who I am. I thank you for making me precious in your eyes." Every time we feel negative about who we are or feel tempted to put ourselves down, we ought to affirm our God-given self-worth with that little prayer. Each of us has to learn to talk back to the negative voices inside and outside of us that threaten our self-worth. We can do this by constantly repeating: "Father, you have made me beautiful in your eyes. I praise you for the wonder of my being."

Second suggestion: We can learn to believe more deeply in our own goodness if we see and receive Jesus in the Eucharist as a tangible sign of his tremendous love for us. At the Last Supper Jesus took bread and said, "This is my body, which will be given for you." Then he took the cup and said, "This cup is the new covenant in my blood, which will be shed for you" (Luke 22:19, 20). In and through these words Jesus is telling each of us: "I am dying that you may live" or "I love you so much that I am ready to pour out my blood (my life) for you." Such words are truly awesome if only we could believe them deeply. Every time we receive Holy Communion, we are being offered an opportunity to affirm our belief in Jesus' love for us. Our "Amen" when we receive the Eucharist at Mass could very well mean "Yes, Lord, I do believe you love me! Help my unbelief."

Third suggestion: We can learn to accept ourselves as good and lovable if we risk sharing our true and false selves with other people. As we begin to reveal our dark or less noble side to another caring person and begin to experience his or her acceptance of us, this acceptance will help us to be more loving toward ourselves. Many people today are finding the therapeutic setting the best and the safest atmosphere in which to make true confessions. Good, caring therapists have both the training and the skills to communicate to their clients their unconditional acceptance. To decide not to reveal all of ourselves to another is to condemn ourselves to a life of loneliness and to be cheated of the opportunity to experience ourselves as unconditionally accepted and loved.

If we truly wish to transform the way we see ourselves, we have to be very patient. If for years we have believed negative and destructive lies about ourselves, we should not expect to change those beliefs overnight. Normally the transformation from a poor to a positive self-concept takes years, and even then we will sometimes find that we occasionally regress into believing negative things about ourselves.

We have treated the love of God and love of self separately in this section. In reality, of course, they are not separate; they are intertwined. As we grow in the experience of God's love, we will also come to see and experience ourselves as lovable.

Questions for Personal Reflection and Small-Group Discussion

1. What spoke to you most in this chapter?
2. When did you come to have a *personal* relationship with God, Jesus, and the Holy Spirit? How did this change your prayer life?
3. What helps you to believe in your own basic goodness? What can threaten or tear down your self-image?
4. What was your experience with the suggested prayer exercise offered below?

Suggested Prayer Exercise

Take time to sit with the three Scripture verses below, and listen to God and Jesus speak words of love to you. Try to visualize Jesus saying to you, "You are precious in my eyes and I love you." Allow time to let these "I love you" statements sink into your heart.

"Because you are precious in my eyes . . . I love you."
(Isaiah 43:4)

"Before I formed you in the womb I knew you,
before you were born I dedicated you." (Jeremiah 1:5)

"As the Father loves me, so I also love you." (John 15:9)

Being Honest with God

Moses again had recourse to the Lord and said,
"Lord, why do you treat this people so badly?
And why did you send me on such a mission?
Ever since I went to Pharaoh to speak in your
name, he has maltreated this people of yours,
and you have done nothing to rescue them.

EXODUS 5:22–23

How often we have mumbled the well-worn formula,
"O my God, I am heartily sorry for having offended
thee, and I detest all my sins because of thy just
punishments. . . ." What [we] really want to say is: "I
am not very sorry for my sins; in fact, I am rather
fond of them, attached to them. I am not afraid of hell
because I know you love me, but I would like to be
different than I am." The point is we need to be honest
before God with what is truly occurring in our life.

KATHERINE DYCKMAN AND PATRICK CARROLL

In the initial stages of a human relationship, we usually make a special effort to be nice to the other person. We tend to avoid talking about issues or feelings that may cause embarrassment or a rift in the relationship. Also, if we are trying to make an impression on the other person, we may make a special effort to come off "looking good." We may use masks to cover up the areas of our personality that we do not like or think the other party wouldn't like. In other words, our tendency will be to edit what we show or reveal to the other. Yet to the extent that we are failing to share our true thoughts and feelings, the relationship is lacking in honesty and genuineness.

For example, we may be angry with a friend but choose not to reveal our feelings of anger. We act as if "everything is just fine," when, in fact, we might be quite angry inside. Such conduct usually has a detrimental effect on the relationship—making it become merely polite, bland, and boring. We begin to talk about external things—like the weather and other people—rather than sharing personal feelings. An atmosphere of "cool distance" replaces intimacy. Often the repressed anger will reveal itself in passive-aggressive behavior. Until the anger is dealt with, the relationship will remain polite and at a cool distance. When the anger is admitted, talked about, and dealt with, the relationship begins to progress and closeness is restored.

For most of us, telling other persons that we are angry with them is far from easy. Very few of us feel comfortable in expressing our anger. Hence, our tendency is to repress our anger and pretend it doesn't exist. Thus the decision to confront difficult feelings or issues in a relationship is a *decision to love*. We make a decision to reach out because we care about the relationship and because we trust in the goodness of the other to understand whatever it is we need to share. In friendships we learn over and over that we enjoy each other's company to the extent that we decide to be honest and genuine with each other.

So it is in our relationship with God. If we are honest and open with God, we will feel close to the Lord most of the time. On the other hand, if we treat God as "polite company," we may find that while we have a "nice" relationship with God, it lacks fire and intimacy. We will probably experience God as a distant figure.

Learning to be open and honest with God is, without a doubt, one of the most difficult lessons that we have to learn in the school of prayer, especially if our tendency in human relationships has been to hide our real thoughts and feelings. It is not easy to tell others, not to mention the Other—God, the perfect One—that we are angry with them or jealous of them or that we don't feel like communicating with them. And yet if the relationship is to grow and mature, that is exactly what we must learn to do.

ADMITTING OUR FEELINGS

Many of us have been taught that being angry at God is a sin. As a consequence we are consciously or unconsciously afraid to tell God that we are angry with him. We may think that if we get angry with God he will strike back and punish us. (Perhaps that was our experience as a child when we got angry with our parents, so we learned to hide and not express our anger.) Spiritual directors tell us that most of us are unconscious of our anger with God. For example, if we think that life is unfair, we may unconsciously blame God and be angry with him for allowing such injustice. In his book, *God and You*, Jesuit priest William Barry writes:

> We might resent being the second-born in the family where it seems the oldest gets all the attention and where we always seem to be second best. We may resent the loss of a parent in childhood through death or divorce. We may have grown up as a member of a harassed minority. We may have a physical deformity or blemishes that have made us the objects of stigmatization by others. *Even if our heads tell us that God is not to blame for these lacks, still they are life's hurts, and the anger and resentment we feel may also be aimed at the Author of life.* At the least, we may at some level feel that God, the all-powerful, could have spared us or protected us if he really loved us.

In the same chapter of that book, Fr. Barry goes on to tell the story of a young woman who had experienced a personal relationship with God. However, since her engagement to be married, she found God to be distant and prayer to be boring. Initially, she did not know the cause of her alienation. It was only gradually and with the help of a spiritual director that she realized that she was very angry that her father, who died when she was five years old, would not be present at her wedding to walk her down the aisle. It was only later still that she realized that she was angry with God that he had taken her father. One day she went to church to thank God for the blessings in her life. But when she tried to pray, images of her wedding flooded her mind. She became enraged that her dad would not be present. She imagined herself going down the aisle alone, showing everyone the terrible thing God had done to her when he took her father. Then she proceeded to express her anger with God in no uncertain terms. Reflecting on her experience, the young lady realized that God had listened to her expression of anger with patience and compassion. The wall between her and God was broken down. God was experienced as closer, and prayer was no longer boring.

An important appendix to the story is that the young lady was not completely freed of her anger during that one prayer experience in church. Periodically, during the weeks following, her anger would flare up anew. Each time this happened she expressed her anger and found that God listened to her patiently and with compassion.

This touching story teaches us several lessons. It teaches us that it is possible to be angry with God about what happened to us years ago. It reminds us about our tendency to repress our anger with God. It shows us that expressing anger at God doesn't drive him away. Instead, it brings him closer to us. Finally, the story teaches us that if we are angry with God about something, we may have to express that anger not just one time but several times.

The prophet Jeremiah can teach us how to be up front with God. Jeremiah was a rather quiet and gentle person, but his "soul-conversations" reveal that sometimes he engaged in some tough dialogues with God. We are very fortunate that his book in the Hebrew Scriptures contains many of his "confessions" or soul-conversations. Being a gentle person, Jeremiah was particularly sensitive to outbursts of hostility from the people he was trying to reach. Once when experiencing such hostility, he cried out in desperation:

> Cursed be the day on which I was born!
> May the day my mother gave me birth never be
> blessed!
> Cursed be the man who brought the news to my father,
> saying,
> "A child, a son, has been born to you!"
> filling him with great joy. (Jeremiah 20:14–15)

In another chapter, Jeremiah complains to God about the injustice of allowing evil people to prosper. He even has some suggestions for God concerning how he ought to deal with the wicked (see Jeremiah 12:1–3).

Jeremiah also questions God about how he treats his servant and wonders if God has been lying to him (see Jeremiah 15:10–21).

For most of us, speaking to God like Jeremiah did is unthinkable. Yet the Scriptures provide many examples of such honest, heartfelt questioning of God and his ways. The Psalms in particular contain many such soul-conversations (see Psalms 22 and 38). The following passages give examples of how open and honest Moses was in his relationship with God: Exodus 5:22–23, Exodus 32:11–14; 30–32, Exodus 33:12–23, Numbers 11:10–15, and Numbers 14:13–19.

We all recognize the fact that even friends become frustrated and angry with each other once in awhile. They get upset when their plans are ignored or when they think their friends are inattentive to their needs and are ignoring them. We must wonder about a relationship where no anger and frustration are experienced. Many spiritual guides tell us that if we are "stuck" in our prayer life, we will often begin to move again when we are able to recognize and express our anger toward God, people, and life.

Several years ago I attended a seminar given by the late Jesuit priest from India, Father Anthony de Mello. In the course of the weekend he told of how he would never forget the night he went to bed telling Jesus he didn't *like him* because he felt he (Jesus) had been pushed on him. He said it was far from easy to express such feelings to Jesus. But the next morning when he got up, he felt better and closer to Jesus. Their relationship was now more real.

It is not only unexpressed anger at God that will cause distance between God and us. We will also create a wall between God and ourselves if we fail to honestly recognize and deal with other feelings that we have toward other people. For example, we may experience feelings of hate, jealousy, fear, lust, guilt, or similar attitudes. As long as such feelings are not dealt with, it is most likely that we will experience a barrier between God and us.

DEALING WITH OUR FEELINGS

Many of us were raised to believe that certain feelings like anger, hate, jealousy, and lust were wrong and sinful. But the good news is that feelings are neither right nor wrong. Rather, feelings, like the clouds (bright or dark), simply exist. There is no such thing as an immoral feeling. *All* feelings, even hate, fear, and jealousy, are good in themselves and have a role to play in our lives. For example, our capacity to feel hate is helpful in the face of sin and evil. We use the feeling of fear to stop us from stepping off a ten-story building. We can have a love that is jealous (in the protective and not possessive sense) for the welfare of our children and loved ones. The question of morality arises only when we express our feelings in inappropriate ways or when we allow our feelings to control our behavior. For example, it is not wrong to have hateful feelings for others. Nor is it wrong to tell them in a kind way that we have feelings of hatred toward them. But it would be wrong for us to allow our feelings of hate to cause us to behave in hateful ways toward others. This can be particularly cruel and confusing when we haven't even told the other person that we are very upset with him or her.

An important part of human and spiritual growth is learning to accept and integrate all of our feelings. We need to be aware of what feelings are unacceptable to us and why. Our so-called negative feelings often flow from some unresolved past hurt or from an upbringing that communicated to us that certain feelings were wrong and bad. If all our lives we have believed that certain feelings (like jealousy, hate, lust, anger, and similar emotions) are wrong or at least unacceptable, it will not be easy for us to move to a point where we easily accept *all* feelings as okay in themselves. It will take time, patience, gentleness, and usually the support of others— including a caring counselor—to help us embrace and treat like a wounded child those feelings in us that we were trained to believe were unacceptable and sinful. This is not a blank check to allow our feelings to control us and run our lives. Rather, it is an exhortation to stop pounding on ourselves for having certain feelings or fantasies. We need to learn how to deal with our feelings as we would deal with a wounded or unruly child—namely, with a combination of gentleness and firmness.

I often use a spiritual journal to help me deal with my tough or uncomfortable feelings. Here are four methods that I use.

First, name the feeling. By simply *naming* an intense feeling that is controlling us, we immediately rob it of some of its power.

Second, express the feelings. If our intense, "negative" feelings are toward a particular person, we should imagine that person sitting opposite us and telling him or her exactly how we feel. We hold nothing back. Actually, the very act of forcefully expressing our true feelings defuses their intensity. It cannot be emphasized enough how important it is to *give expression* to our feelings *before* we pray for their healing.

Third, own the feelings and accept them as part of who we are. It is not easy for any of us to admit that sometimes we have feelings of jealousy, inadequacy, hate, and so forth. Each of us probably has our own list of feelings that we particularly find very difficult to accept. Much of the shadowy, unconscious side of our personalities consists of feelings that we judge to be unacceptable. The result is that we push such feelings into our unconscious and refuse to relate to them. Unfortunately, such feelings, like an unruly child, continue to exert a negative influence in our lives and will continue to do so until we enter into a reconciling relationship with them.

One way for us to grow in our acceptance and ownership of our unacceptable feelings is by dialoguing with them as we would dialogue with an unruly child or a friend with whom we have had a disagreement. We can use our imagination to personify the internal feeling with which we want to dialogue. We can give the feeling a name (call him "Red Anger" or her "Jealous Susie") and imagine him or her sitting down opposite us. We might begin the dialogue in this fashion:

You/Self: I hate admitting that you are a part of my household. I just hate the control that you sometimes have over me. I also hate the way you make me feel inside.

Red Anger: I know how much you dislike me and wish I didn't exist. Nevertheless I am glad that you have finally decided to take a few minutes to talk to me. For so long you have ignored me and pushed me away into some dark corner of your heart.

You/Self: You're right. I have ignored you, and a part of me even now wants to continue to ignore you. Frankly, I just hate to think that you are a part of me, and that is why I usually push you away when you show yourself. Yet I know for my own peace and integration that I must recognize your presence, learn to talk to you, and even befriend you.

Red Anger: Good. I'm delighted that you want to talk to me. I know that I can cause you much grief—especially in that part of you that likes always to be in control. Perhaps my presence and intensity wouldn't be so bad if you learned not to panic when I appear on the scene. Instead, just be there for me—listen to me as you would listen to a friend who is very angry or to a child who is upset about something.

You/Self: You know, Red Anger, I feel better already. Just the act of recognizing your presence and talking to you defuses a lot of heat and replaces it with feelings of peace and quiet. Perhaps you are not the horrible creature I thought you were, and if I would give you a little more recognition and attention, you would not create such havoc inside of me.

This conversation is a concrete example of how we can begin to bring peace and reconciliation to feelings and parts of us that we would rather ignore. We all know that we feel better when we choose to talk to an enemy in our external lives. Why should it be any different with our internal enemies? Each of us has a number of them (skeletons in the closet) whose existence we have never admitted, let alone dialogued with. Jesus commands us to love our enemies (see Luke 6:27–36). But what if our biggest enemies live within? Growth and integration as human and spiritual persons involve learning to relate to our inner voices, feelings, and figures—learning to befriend the enemy within. Whenever we take the time to engage in such dialogue, we invariably feel more peaceful and integrated. We feel like we do after we have decided to talk to a friend with whom we have had a falling out. (Two good books to read about dialoguing and healing our feelings are: Morton Kelsey's *The Adventure Inward* and *The Other Side of Silence.*)

Fourth, talk to Jesus about these feelings and seek his healing. It is important and consoling to remember that Jesus, being fully human, probably experienced at times all the feelings with which we feel uncomfortable. In fact, it is very helpful if we can find and reflect on an incident in Scripture where Jesus had a feeling similar to ours. For example, if we feel angry we can meditate on the Temple scene where Jesus became angry with the buyers and sellers (see John 2:13–22). In praying to the Lord about our feelings, we might ask him to help us see why a particular encounter or event sparked off certain feelings in us. Perhaps we feel jealous of someone else's gifts because we are unaware or unappreciative of our own gifts.

Perhaps we got very angry with someone because he or she told us a truth we didn't want to hear. When we find within ourselves uncaring feelings for another person, we need to ask Jesus to give us a new heart toward that person (see Psalm 51).

Of course, learning to be honest with God involves more than dealing with uncomfortable feelings. Dealing with our feelings, especially the feeling of anger, has been made the main focus of this section because it is an area in which most of us have received very little spiritual guidance, and often the guidance we received was, unfortunately, more destructive than helpful to our human and spiritual growth.

In summary, we need to realize that learning to be real and honest with God involves bringing our whole selves before God: our messy selves, our confused selves, our good selves. It involves learning to talk to God about our relationships, our jobs, our possessions, our sexiest, wildest, most cruel thoughts, feelings, fantasies, and desires. It involves talking to God about our money: how we make it and how we spend it. It involves talking to God about how we use our time and talents. If we really want to know what is important to us, all we need to do is check and see how we use our time, treasure, and talents.

Honesty in prayer will involve bringing before the Lord our doubts, fears, and the anger we may have toward God, others, and self. It may involve telling God that we are sorry for some sins but not so sorry for others, at least at this time. It may involve telling God that we are not yet ready to surrender to him certain areas of our lives. Such openness and honesty about our real self will not happen overnight. It will take time and usually the support and encouragement of a soul-friend. In fact, we are only truly genuine with ourselves, others, and God on rare occasions. But we should treasure such moments because they are moments of true encounter. Honesty with God, others, and self demands a huge amount of courage and humility. We ought to pray frequently for such courage and humility.

Questions for Personal Reflection and Small-Group Discussion

1. What spoke to you most in the chapter?
2. Do you tend to treat God as "polite company," or do you tend to level with God about the important matters in your life?
3. Why do you think people would hesitate to talk to God about certain parts of their lives? Why might you hesitate?
4. Have you ever risked an honest "moment" with God like the example given by Anthony de Mello in this section? If so, what happened? How did it feel?
5. What was your experience with the suggested prayer exercise offered below?

Suggested Prayer Exercise

Choose an area or feeling in your life about which you have never talked to God. Write a letter to the Lord about this forgotten or "forbidden" area or feeling. Then try to jot down what you think God's response to you might be. Later, have a dialogue with one of your troublesome feelings in a way similar to what was demonstrated on pages 38–39.

Connecting Prayer With Daily Life

Be doers of the word and not hearers only . . .

JAMES 1:22

Unless the prayers we speak are tightly linked with the lives we lead, they will be babblings we hide behind rather than true speech which reveals who we are in relation to all that is.

JOHN SHEA

One of the biggest challenges of the spiritual journey is the integration of prayer (our relationship with God) to the rest of life. Most of us, particularly men, have a tendency to compartmentalize life. We give sections of our day to work, family, and recreation, and only then do we allot to God a portion (too often a leftover portion) of our day. There is, of course, a real sense in which we need to compartmentalize the activities of our day if we are to properly concentrate on each activity.

From a spiritual point of view, however, such compartmentalization would be very destructive if it meant the exclusion of the Lord from the secular activities of our day. If Jesus is to become *Lord* of our life, he must be invited to guide and permeate every activity of our day. When this happens our whole day—with its religious and secular dimensions—will become one act of worship to the Father. Jesuit priest Richard Hauser, in his book entitled *In His Spirit: A Guide to Today's Spirituality*, writes: "The holiest actions of our day are those done most in tune with the Spirit: These may be either prayer or service."

Authentic spirituality does not separate formal prayer and secular activities because the same Spirit is present and active in all of them. Ideally one complements the other. True prayer imbues our action with the Spirit of Christ, and action done in God's Spirit not only sanctifies us but also prepares us for formal prayer.

The spiritual life is all of life: cooking, paying bills, driving to work and Little League games, making love, and dealing with conflicts. God isn't just present in the "holy things" such as the Eucharist, the Church, and the Bible. God is present in all encounters, events, and objects. Moses met God in a burning bush. Every bush or event in life is burning with the presence of God, if only we have the faith to see it. The challenge is not just to do a few spiritual exercises every week when we attend Mass, read the Bible, or pray the Rosary. The challenge is to make every encounter and event of our week a spiritual exercise through which we grow in our relationship with God. The more we do this, the more real God will become for us. God will become a companion with whom we share all of life—not like a doctor whom we call when we need some help or a boss with whom we exchange daily greetings and niceties but with whom there is no personal relationship. The more we compartmentalize God and box him in, the more unreal he will be to us and the more we will be alienated from him. Perhaps one reason why God allows our prayer life to dry up is because we have stopped looking for the Lord in the laundry room, the store, or the office.

INTEGRATION THROUGH OCCUPATIONAL AND SPOUSAL PRAYER

How do we go about integrating prayer with our daily life? One way is to make careful use of what William McNamara, OCD, in his book, *The Human Adventure*, calls occupational and spousal prayer. Occupational prayer takes place while we are on the job of daily living. Spousal prayer happens when we rest from all activity so that we can be totally present and available to God, our Divine Spouse. (Notice that spousal prayer describes our relationship to God as our spouse and does not refer to one's marital status or state in life.) Both forms of prayer—occupational and spousal—are important and interdependent. One feeds into and needs the other.

Occupational prayer is the daily dialogue we have with God as we go about the daily tasks of life and behold the beauty of creation. We accept the fact that the spiritual life encompasses all of life. Occupational prayer makes that statement a reality in our lives. It is the kind of prayer that can give quality and power to the mundane, pedestrian affairs of life. When we pray as we go about the work of our day, God will be our partner in cooking meals, changing diapers, conducting business affairs, playing tennis, making hospital calls, driving the car—whatever we do on the occupational level.

Author Susan Muto, in *Pathways in Spiritual Living*, describes her occupational prayer in this way:

> Morning dawns. I awaken slowly and take an extra moment to say thanks to God for the gift of this day. While dressing, I try to center my thoughts on the Lord: "Even if I do not think of you explicitly, let me do what I do for your sake." I eat and feel grateful for the food on my table. While driving, I can still take a few moments for recollection. I stop at the traffic light and look over the hills, knowing that his presence is everywhere. I intersperse mental plans for my morning with brief meditations on his providential care.

> . . . By the time I arrive at the office, my working day has already taken on a deeper meaning. What might have been a merely functional approach is replaced by a rhythmic blend of action and contemplation, labor and leisure and all because of a shift in attitude. . . .

For occupational prayer to have depth, it will need to be backed up with regular periods of spousal prayer. Sometimes the popular slogan, "My work is my prayer," is used as an excuse for not setting aside time for spousal prayer. This is indeed an unfortunate error in spiritual living that keeps our relationship with the Lord superficial. Spiritual directors all agree that only by seeking to be exclusively present to the Lord through spousal prayer on a regular basis will we grow in our ability to be present to God all of the time through occupational prayer. The document *Spiritual Renewal of the American Priesthood* (published by the United States Catholic Conference) reminds us that when everything is prayer, nothing is prayer, and without prayer we perish. When we attempt to find God everywhere but in no particular place, we tend to find him nowhere. Those who pray on the job also need to enter their room and pray to their Father in secret.

The quality of our presence to the encounters and activities of daily life will be in direct proportion to the quality of our presence to God who is the Ground of all presence.

The importance of regular periods of exclusive time with the Lord (that is, spousal prayer) cannot be stressed too much. Unfortunately most people seem to lack conviction about the pressing need for regular periods of spousal prayer. Yet if Jesus and all the saints through the ages found the need for regular periods of spousal prayer, surely we lesser mortals should be able to see our need for such times of prayer.

I often remind people that there are 1,440 minutes in every day and ninety-six fifteen-minute periods. Then I ask:

"Can you truthfully say you are serious about your relationship with God if you do not give one or two of the ninety-six fifteen-minute periods in every day to God or twenty or thirty of the 1,440 minutes?" Then I continue: "If at this time in your spiritual journey, giving the Lord fifteen or thirty minutes a day is not part of your daily schedule, I suggest that you reflect on why it isn't."

PRETEXTS FOR NOT INTEGRATING

Some people are fearful of integrating their prayer life with their daily life. Here are some of the excuses they use:

"I'm too busy." This certainly is true for most of us. We feel overscheduled to death. Yet the deeper issue is the lack of conviction about the vital importance of spousal prayer for our spiritual health and growth. Isn't it remarkable how people with kidney problems and with very busy schedules make time for two-hour visits to the hospital three times a week for dialysis? None of these people would ever dream of saying to the doctor, "Sorry, doctor, I can't do it; I'm too busy." We always have time for what is important to us.

"Formal or spousal prayer is just for priests and religious and very dedicated laypeople, but not for the ordinary Catholic." The truth is that *all* God's children are called to a life of holiness. The bishops assembled for the Second Vatican Council in the early 1960s stressed that the call to holiness is universal.

The Lord Jesus . . . preached holiness of life to each and every one of his disciples regardless of their situation. . . . All the faithful of Christ of whatever rank or status are called to the fullness of Christian life and to the perfection of charity (*Dogmatic Constitution on the Church*, 40).

"I'd have no idea of how to spend twenty minutes of quiet time with the Lord." This is actually true for most laypeople—hence, the importance of books like this.

"I used to have a daily quiet time, but I quit because I felt I was making no progress, going nowhere." This reveals the problem of dryness, which will be dealt with in chapter thirteen.

"I don't want to get too serious about prayer because—consciously or unconsciously—I'm afraid of losing control over my life." At the heart of authentic prayer is surrender to the will of God. Because we fear this surrender and where it leads—to the cross—most of us keep God at arm's length. We may frequently "say prayers" or read Scripture often, but we may not listen properly because we are afraid of giving God control over our lives.

"I don't want to listen too closely to God in prayer because I'm afraid of what the Lord might say to me." He might ask something of us that we are not ready to give, or he may reveal to us something about ourselves that we would prefer not to hear. All the spiritual masters tell us that growth in self-knowledge is an essential ingredient of human and spiritual growth. We all create a certain ideal image of ourselves that we try very hard to protect. We are not very open to allowing God an

opportunity to crack that ideal self-image by revealing to us a less perfect side. Also, most of us are afraid of being found by God. Like Adam and Eve, we often hide when we think God is coming our way (see Genesis 3:8).

Building into our schedules a regular quiet time with the Lord is, without doubt, one of the most important actions we can perform to facilitate our spiritual growth. It is not, however, an easy discipline to develop. Most people who give the Lord a special quiet time on a regular basis will witness to the fact that it took much cooperation with God's grace to develop the discipline of spousal prayer. Most of us need the encouragement and the reinforcement of a spiritual director or a small group of soul-friends to begin and maintain a conviction about the value of regular times of spousal prayer with God.

If spousal prayer is presently not a part of our prayer life, we can begin now to ask God to place in our hearts a desire to spend a daily quiet time with him. Then, as we feel led, we can begin to spend fifteen to twenty minutes of daily quiet time with him. Part Two of this book will offer some suggestions on how to spend a quiet time with the Lord. (One of the best tools to help us integrate prayer and life is the Consciousness Examen explained in chapter six.)

Questions for Personal Reflection and Small-Group Discussion

1. What spoke to you most in this chapter?
2. Does your relationship with God presently include regular times of spousal prayer? If not, why not? If so, how did you come to a conviction about the importance of spousal prayer and how do you usually spend that time?
3. What problems do you face as you try to integrate prayer or gospel values with the rest of your life? What helps and hinders you in this challenge?
4. What was your experience with the suggested prayer exercise offered below?

Suggested Prayer Exercise

Take Jesus on a tour of your life. Invite him to enter every area: work, relationships, finances, sexuality, recreation, prayer, whatever. Try to speak to him honestly about each one of these. Notice the times when you feel happy and comfortable with him, and notice the times when you feel awkward, hesitant, and uncomfortable. Be in touch with the feelings you experience as you move from one area to another.

Listening to God in Prayer

Oh, that today you would hear his voice:
Harden not your hearts....

Psalm 95:7–8

To listen is much more difficult than to speak. When
we speak we are the center of attention. We enjoy
this. However, when we listen the other becomes
the center of attention and that is much more
demanding. To listen means that ... we must empty
ourselves in order to be filled with the other person.
[In prayer] listening implies being open
to what God wants to do in us and also
being ready to respond to God.

David E. Rosage

In the verse of Scripture quoted above, God is pleading with Israel to listen to his voice and direction. Because they often refused to listen to God, the Israelite people brought much hardship on themselves and were not as close to God as they could have been. They spent many years journeying a few miles in the desert. The journey would have taken them a much shorter time if they had learned to hear and obey God's leading and direction.

One of the main reasons why many of us make slow progress in the spiritual life is that we never develop an inner spiritual ear with which to listen to the leadings of God's Holy Spirit. In his book, *Opening to God*, Jesuit priest Thomas Green writes:

> Listening is a real art which some people never learn. We all have experienced people who cannot or do not listen. They hear but they do not understand; their bodily ears pick up sound, but their hearts are not attentive to its meaning. . . . The good pray-er is above all a good listener.

We should not try to dominate the time we spend with God. In the Scriptures we read where the young boy Samuel says to God, "Speak, Lord, for your servant is listening" (1 Samuel 3:10). It seems many of us have misread that text, thinking that it says, "Listen, Lord, your servant is speaking." So often in prayer we speak too much and listen too little. In theory we may believe that what God has to say to us is much more important than what we have to say to God, but in practice we act as if what we have to say is the more important of the two. We rush into our place of prayer, say our prayers, do our reading, and then rush away without ever giving God any chance to speak to us. If we treated our friends like this, we would lose them. God created us with two ears and one mouth, hoping perhaps that we would listen twice as much as we would speak. If that was God's intention, not very many of us got the message.

NECESSARY ATTITUDES FOR LISTENING

True listening in prayer is a real challenge, demanding faith, selflessness, patience, a reflective attitude, and courage.

We need *faith* to believe that God does communicate with us, his people; and we especially need faith to believe that God really does want to speak to us personally.

We need *selflessness* because listening always demands the ability and willingness to put aside our own need to talk or our desire to be center stage, so that we can listen to others and give them center stage.

We need *patience* because God does not always speak to us according to our time schedule. He tells us so himself, "Nor are your ways my ways" (Isaiah 55:8).

We need to develop a *reflective attitude* toward life so we can learn to read God's messages as they come to us in the events and encounters of daily life.

And, of course, true listening demands *courage* because God sometimes asks us to travel places we'd prefer not to go. Remember the story of Jonah who took the first ship out of port to get away from God (see Jonah 1:1—2:11). Recall what Jesus himself said to Peter at the end: "When you grow old... someone else will dress you and lead you where you do not want to go" (John 21:18).

We should pray often for a *desire* to hear God's voice and for the above-mentioned dispositions that enable us to hear and respond to the Word of God. In the spiritual life *all is gift*. Hence we must constantly pray for the dispositions of heart that will facilitate our growth in Christ.

In his book, *Opening to God*, Fr. Green titles chapter two "The Irrelevance of Prayer" and chapter three "The Relevance of Prayer." When I first read the title of chapter two, I was somewhat taken aback. I wondered how anyone (especially a priest) could speak about the irrelevance of prayer. After all, isn't any type of prayer always relevant? So I couldn't wait to read the chapters to see what Fr. Green meant. When I had finished reading both chapters, I discovered his meaning.

Fr. Green explains that prayer is irrelevant when it is merely our attempt to get God to do what we want—to get God to do our will. On the other hand, prayer is very relevant when it is our attempt to discover what God wants of us and our attempt to seek the strength to carry out his will.

If our primary goal in prayer is to let God know our needs and to ask him to take care of them, we run the risk of developing a kind of professional relationship with God, not a personal one. We will see God simply as one who can take care of some of our needs. When we go to see a professional person—let's say our doctor—we are just interested in the services that he can render to us. We are not there to develop a personal relationship with him. It is different with people we call friends. We do not visit them primarily to take care of some business. Rather, we visit with them so that we can deepen our friendship. We may listen to them, they may listen to us, or we may simply enjoy each other's presence. In other words, the primary focus is not to obtain a service but to deepen a friendship.

The Lord wants us to regard him as a friend with whom we would want to "waste time," someone to whom we willingly listen (see John 15:15 and Matthew 11:28–30). It would be sad if we treated God as a "Divine Do-Gooder" whom we called on only in time of need. If we are to develop a personal relationship with the Lord, we must be willing not only to open our hearts to God about our needs but also to sit quietly at the feet of the Master so that he can speak to us (see Luke 10:38–42).

HOW GOD SPEAKS TO US

Presuming we are interested in making prayer a time when we primarily listen for the voice of God, our question might be, "How does God speak to us?" After all, no one has ever seen God or heard his voice the way we have heard the voice of friends. God uses many channels to speak to us. He speaks to us through sunrises and sunsets, through a smiling face, through sickness patiently endured, through the needy beggar. He speaks to us especially through sacred writings, through the lives of other people, through the events of daily life, and through his creation. This can be seen in the following personal examples.

Through sacred writings: God can speak through a sacred or inspired text. Recall the Gospel for the Feast of All Saints, which focuses on the Beatitudes (see Matthew 5:1–12). In pondering and dwelling on this text for a few minutes, I could practically hear the Lord saying to me, "Saints are people who live the Beatitudes. They don't just read about them or tell others about them. They actually live each Beatitude." I especially felt the Lord say to me, "Saints are, above all, single-minded in their approach to life. They seek me above and in all things." This was a simple but beautiful message that encouraged me to be more vigilant in my seeking of God. The next time I read this text God may say something different to me, for the Word of God is inexhaustible.

Through the lives of other people: God can speak through the words of other people or through the quiet witness of their lives. In our parish, we have many parishioners who spend a lot of time each week responding to the needs of the needy in our area. Their dedication is a reminder to me that I too must be concerned about the needs of the least of our brothers and sisters. Jesus often speaks to us through the witness of other people's lives. We just need to be alert for what he may be saying to us.

Through the events of daily life: God can and does speak through the events of daily life. A few years ago, while driving on an interstate highway, my car skidded on the wet road and crashed into a wall. I was very fortunate that I did not injure either myself or anyone else. Without reflecting on the event, I could simply have said, "Boy, I was pretty lucky," and then proceeded to see about the repair of my car. But by prayerfully reflecting on the event, it was as if God said to me: "Eamon, you need to drive more carefully on wet roads. This should remind you of how fragile and vulnerable human life is. The best way to thank me for the daily gift of life is to live it fully but with proper caution." Although I heard God say this to me, he might have spoken a different message to someone else in the same situation.

Through God's creation: God can speak to us through the majesty and beauty of his creation. Elizabeth Barrett Browning, in her poem entitled "Aurora Leigh," puts it this way:

> Earth's crammed with heaven,
> And every common bush afire with God;
> But only he who sees takes off his shoes;
> The rest sit round it and pluck blackberries.

In Melbourne, Florida, I live ten minutes from the Atlantic Ocean. It is difficult to walk the beach and not see in it a reflection of the Creator. The big, mighty waves of the ocean hurrying toward the seashore and the lovely sunrises speak to me of the power, the majesty, and the beauty of God.

Such "reading into" or interpreting the events and encounters of life might seem rather strange to some people, yet to the person of faith it is perfectly normal. The eighteenth-century spiritual director, Jean-Pierre de Caussade, in his book, *Abandonment to Divine Providence*, writes:

> There is never a moment when God does not come forward in the guise of some suffering or some duty, and all that takes place within, around us, and through us both includes and hides his activity. . . . If we could lift the veil and if we watched with vigilant attention, God would endlessly reveal himself to us. . . . It is faith which interprets God for us. Without its light we should not even know that God was speaking but would hear only the confused, meaningless babble of creatures. As Moses saw the flame of fire in the bush and heard the voice of God coming from it, so faith will enable us to understand his hidden signs, so that amidst all the apparent clutter and disorder we shall see all the loveliness and perfection of divine wisdom.

Now, we may ask how we know that we are hearing God's voice and not just hearing or reading into events what we want to hear or read. This certainly is an important question because we humans have quite a facility for making God say to us what we want him to say.

Learning to hear and discern the voice of God is both a gift and an art. It is a gift of the Holy Spirit which we need to receive frequently and an art to learn by trial and error (see 1 Corinthians 12:10). Getting to know the voice of God is somewhat like getting to know the voice of a newfound friend. At first we do not readily recognize our friend's voice on the phone. But as the friendship grows, we recognize the person's voice as soon as we hear the word *hello*. If we live our lives in the company of Jesus, we will become more and more familiar with his voice. (Later in this book, when we discuss the Prayer of Consciousness Examen, we will consider another excellent way to grow in our ability to hear, discern, and respond to the voice of our God.)

Questions for Personal Reflection and Small-Group Discussion

1. What spoke to you most in this chapter?
2. Can you share an experience in which you felt God's presence and direction?
3. This chapter names four ways that God seeks to communicate with us. To what extent can you identify with one or more of these channels of God's outreach to his people?
4. What was your experience with the suggested prayer exercise offered below?

Suggested Prayer Exercise

Tomorrow make a special effort to be attentive to any messages that God may wish to send you through reading, persons, events, or creation. At the end of the day take a minute or two to jot down the messages you think you received from God.

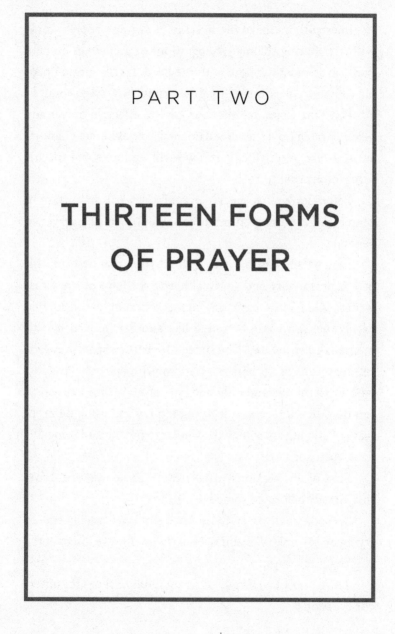

PART TWO

THIRTEEN FORMS OF PRAYER

At times authors make the mistake of urging people to pray without offering them any suggestions or guidelines on how they can spend quiet time with the Lord. It's like urging people to swim and assuming that they know how to go about it.

Part One examined the four keys to effective prayer and demonstrated how these fundamentals are extremely important to every prayer life. Part Two will explore some specific forms of praying.

Before looking at specific prayer styles, it is important to keep in mind some pertinent facts about forms of prayer in general.

Each person has to discover the rhythm that best suits his or her personality and spiritual needs. St. John of the Cross writes: "God leads each one along different paths so that hardly one spirit will be found like another in even half its method or procedure." The sixteenth-century Spanish mystic reserves some of his harshest criticisms for spiritual directors who insist on one and only one type of prayer for every person they direct. In a way, learning to pray and using different ways of praying are somewhat similar to buying and using different pairs of shoes.

First of all, we don't usually think about wearing shoes that already belong to someone else.

Second, when we go to the shoe store, we usually end up trying on several styles and sizes of shoes until we discover the pair that fits us best.

Third, most people buy different kinds of shoes for different occasions.

Fourth, we may buy a pair of shoes that we don't particularly like and that doesn't even fit very well, yet these shoes eventually may become one of our favorite pairs.

In a similar way, this is true of our prayer life.

First: We should not try to pray in a particular way just because this way works for or fits someone else.

Second: We should try several forms of prayer until we discover the ones that best suit our temperament, spiritual needs, and schedules.

Third: It is wise to be familiar with a variety of prayer forms that we can use at different times.

Fourth: We may sometimes find ourselves feeling very comfortable with a form of prayer that initially felt very awkward for us.

Like shoes, forms of prayer are a means to an end; therefore, we should use them in a way that best serves our needs. During any of our daily prayer periods, we may use several forms of prayer.

ONE

Prayer of Thanksgiving

*Ten were cleansed, were they not? Where are
the other nine? Has none but this foreigner
returned to give thanks to God?*

<small>LUKE 17:17–18</small>

*Father, all powerful and ever-living God,
we do well always and everywhere to give you thanks.
You have no need of our praise, yet our desire to thank
you is itself your gift. Our prayer of thanksgiving
adds nothing to your greatness, but makes us grow
in your grace, through Jesus Christ our Lord.*

<small>WEEKDAY MASS PREFACE, ROMAN MISSAL, 1973</small>

In the prayer of thanksgiving, we give gratitude to God for his loving activity in creation, in the lives of others, and in our own lives. The words of the preface indicate that God has no need of our thanks in the way that we need stroking and affirmation. Yet we can safely assume that our prayers and deeds of thanks do please God. Even more, we know that developing a grateful heart toward God is beneficial to our mental and spiritual well-being. When we take time out to recognize and give thanks to God for what is good in life, we not only recognize God as the Source of all good things, but we also grow in our experience of God as a loving and generous Person. In turn, this experience of God will probably lead us to a more generous giving of ourselves to God. In short, our acts of gratitude to God deepen our relationship with God—hence, the vital importance of taking time out for the prayer of thanksgiving.

We show extreme ingratitude when we take little or no time to identify God's gifts or blessings and rarely give thanks. Worse still, we may believe that the blessings in life are just the result of our own hard work and ingenuity. Moses sternly warned the Israelites not to have that attitude toward the blessings of God. He tells them:

> You then become haughty of heart and unmindful of the Lord, your God, who brought you out of the land of Egypt, that place of slavery; who guided you through the vast and terrible desert . . . who . . . fed you in the desert with manna. . . . Otherwise, you might say to yourselves, "It is my own power and the strength of my own hand that has obtained for me this wealth." Remember then, it is the Lord, your God, who gives you the power to acquire wealth. (Deuteronomy 8:14–18)

Moses is reminding the Israelites never to forget the gratitude they owe to the one who is the Source of their blessings.

When we take little or no time out to give thanks to God, we may begin to think that God is more or less absent from our lives. When we lose the connection between God and the good things in life, we run the risk of losing our relationship with God—period. We will perceive God as distant and uninvolved in our lives.

The prayer of thanksgiving not only enhances our relationship with God, but it also helps our own general sense of well-being. The grateful person is usually a happy person, and the grumbling person is usually unhappy. The priest/sociologist, Andrew Greeley, in his book, *The Bottom-Line Catechism*, writes:

> The empirical research my colleagues and I have done confirms the age-old Christian tradition that prayers of gratitude are the most important, for the relationship between prayer and mental health and marital satisfaction seems to be true only for those whose frequent prayers are prayers of thanksgiving. Prayer brings psychological peace and personal happiness precisely insofar as it becomes a grateful response to a gift of love that is perceived as having already been given.

World-famous catechist, Jesuit priest Johannes Hofinger, in his book, *Pastoral Life in the Power of the Spirit,* has written:

> Lack of gratitude is always a clear sign of selfishness, and selfishness is the hotbed of all kinds of emotional dis-

turbances. Genuine, deep gratitude, on the other hand, opens man in a healthy way toward others; it always helps him to overcome an unhealthy concentration upon himself and it has, by its very nature, a tremendous power of interior healing.

All of this impresses on us the importance of developing a grateful spirit and shows us the potential destructiveness of an ungrateful spirit. A spirit of gratefulness deepens our relationship with God; it increases our mental well-being and helps us to be happier people.

St. Paul exhorts us: "Rejoice always. Pray without ceasing. In all circumstances give thanks" (1 Thessalonians 5:16–18). Does this mean that we are supposed to thank God for the painful and evil things that happen to us? Surely God does not expect or want us to give thanks for the evil things that happen to us or others. But we can and should thank God for his presence and help in times of evil and pain. We can also give thanks to God for the way he is able to bring good out of evil. No doubt all of us can tell stories of how God turned the tables on evil and used the event to teach us some valuable lesson or bring us closer to him.

In all this we need to be aware that one danger in this form of prayer is repression of unpleasant emotions. We may first need to grieve the losses we suffer or feel and then express our feelings of anger and frustration before we praise God and open our hearts to the joy and peace that this brings with it.

How then should we give thanks to God for his blessings? We can do this in countless ways. Here are a few suggestions.

The Mass is the great prayer of thanksgiving for Catholic Christians. The word *Eucharist* means "thanksgiving." We can attend a weekday Mass and use it as our prayer of thanksgiving for some particular blessing in our lives.

We can use the five decades of the Rosary to give thanks to God for five specific blessings in our lives. It can't be emphasized enough how important it is to actually name what we think are the blessings in our lives.

We can give thanks by sharing our blessings with others. For example, we could thank the Lord for the blessing of health by becoming a blood donor or by visiting the sick or shut-ins of our community. We could thank the Lord for material blessings by sharing those blessings with the poor.

As we walk through any given day, we can whisper or shout aloud a word of thanks to the Lord.

We can also compose a personal litany of the things we are grateful for in life.

Questions for Personal Reflection and Small-Group Discussion

1. What spoke to you most in this chapter?
2. Name the top five things you are most grateful for.
3. In your experience, how true is it to say that the practice of thanking God for specific gifts leads you to a greater sense of God's love and presence in your life and helps you to be a happier person?
4. What was your experience of the suggested prayer exercise offered below?

Suggested Prayer Exercise

Make a list of the good things in life you are grateful for that you may be inclined to take for granted. Also try to get in touch with some events in your present life for which you would find it very hard to be grateful. Try to give thanks to God for all the happenings in your life, trusting that as you reach beyond your feelings, God will bless you.

TWO

Prayer of Petition

*And I tell you, ask and you will receive; seek and you
will find; knock and the door will be opened to you. . . .
If you then, who are wicked, know how to give good
gifts to your children, how much more will the Father
in heaven give the holy Spirit to those who ask him?*

LUKE 11:9, 13

*The power of prayer to obtain graces does not
depend on our merits but on the mercy of God. But
the graces that we ask for must be graces related
to our eternal welfare. We may ask for temporal
goods, but they must be asked for only on the
condition that they will be of benefit to our souls.*

ST. ALPHONSUS LIGUORI

For most of us the prayer of petition is not only the most common but also the most intriguing and mysterious of all types
of prayer. We probably have several questions about how this
prayer works. We may wonder why we have the prayer of petition—period. Doesn't God know what we need? Why should

we offer him any suggestions on how to improve people and the world in which we live? In the prayer of petition, are we trying to clue God in on what he might otherwise have over-looked? Does our prayer of petition move God to do things he otherwise had not planned to do? Why did Jesus heal the son of the widow of Nain immediately (see Luke 7:11–17) and wait for twenty years or so to answer St. Monica's prayer for the conversion of her son Augustine? Why does God seem-ingly not answer some prayers—for example, those for the healing of a young mother who eventually dies of cancer? On the lighter side, we might ask: "What does God do when the Miami Dolphins are playing a football game against the Dallas Cowboys and the fans of both teams are praying that their team wins?"

Trying to explain the nature of petitionary prayer and how it works is a theological problem to which there is no satisfactory answer. In groping with this problem, we are try-ing to understand the ways of God and how God works in our world. St. Paul realizes the complexity of this question and writes: "Oh, the depth of the riches and wisdom and knowl-edge of God! How inscrutable are his judgments and how unsearchable his ways! For who has known the mind of the Lord?" (Romans 11:33–34). For most—if not all—of the great theologians and saints who have struggled with questions about how petitionary prayer works, the bottom line is simi-lar to that of Job who finally admitted his inability to solve the mystery of suffering. He told the Lord that he had been trying to solve things too big for him (see Job 40:3–5).

Yet it is legitimate for the curious-minded among us to probe the mystery of petitionary prayer so we can live with it a little more intelligently and a little less anxiously. One helpful insight comes from an article by William Whalen in a September, 1983, *U.S. Catholic* article entitled "How Catholic Prayer Became a Mass Movement":

The prayer of petition is part of God's plan for man. When we say that God answers prayers we do not mean that prayer can cause God to change his mind. God has made the whole world and governs it with his providence. Everything that occurs in the world takes place according to his plan. But it is part of God's plan that certain gifts will be given to man only in answer to prayer. We pray not to change God's plans, but in order to receive from God those things which he has planned to give us in answer to our prayers.

Our daily experiences seem to bear out the basic truth of this statement. There are some gifts we give to others without their asking. Other gifts we give only when we are asked. In waiting to act in response to our prayers or until we petition him, God is allowing us to participate in our own salvation and the salvation of others. Also, the purpose of petitionary prayer is not to inform God of our needs but rather to inform ourselves. Petitionary prayer deepens our awareness of how much we need God at every moment of our lives. When we pray in this way, we can always expect some change in ourselves, if not in the external circumstances which prompted our prayer. We can always expect God to give us the strength to deal with the circumstances of our lives even if he does not change them. This seemingly was the experience of the author of Psalm 138, who writes:

> When I called, you answered me; you built up strength within me. (Psalm 138:3)

What the psalmist is telling us is that "having God answer our prayers" sometimes involves "having him build up his strength" in us. While we may not understand the how of petitionary prayer, we should have no doubt about its importance. God does want us to express our petitions, and he does answer these prayers, even if not in the exact way we wanted. The Our Father, the prayer Jesus taught his disciples, is basically a prayer of petition, particularly the second part of it. Many verses in the psalms also express belief in the prayer of petition:

> Blessed be the Lord, for he has heard the sound of my pleading. (Psalm 28:6)

> When I call out to the LORD, he answers me from his holy mountain. (Psalm 3:5)

We should never become so sophisticated in our spiritual life that we feel petitionary prayer is beneath us. Thinking this would imply that we have outgrown our need for God. We will always need the prayer of petition because we will always need to express our dependence on God. Of course, as we mature in prayer and learn to trust more in God's inscrutable ways, our attitude toward petitionary prayer will change. It will become more God-centered and less self-centered.

PROPER ATTITUDES FOR PETITIONARY PRAYER

There are two important attitudes to bring to the prayer of petition. We must be aware that God is certainly interested in our prayer, and we must realize that the primary purpose of the prayer of petition is to deepen our relationship with God.

Awareness of God's interest: When we petition God in prayer, we are not trying to contact Someone who already has a full "case load" and is therefore just not interested in "another case." God is present, active, and intensely interested in all of his creation. He is the origin (and the sustainer) of all things, drawing and guiding all to their omega point. Creation—of which we are a part—is God's big project. God is passionately concerned that it evolves and develops according to his plan. About this plan St. Paul tells us:

He chose us in him, before the foundation of the world, to be holy and without blemish before him. In love he destined us for adoption to himself through Jesus Christ.

> . . . He has made known to us the mystery of his will in
> accord with his favor that he set forth in him as a plan
> for the fullness of times, to sum up all things in Christ,
> in heaven and on earth. (Ephesians 1:4–5; 9–10)

In our vulnerable and weak moments, we may doubt and even disbelieve God's interest in creation. Often it may seem to us that God is on a "long vacation," is "off duty," or is frequently "out to lunch." When we think such human thoughts, we should reinforce our faith with the knowledge that God has already proved his passionate interest in the most radical way possible—through the life, death, and resurrection of Jesus. "No one has greater love than this, to lay down one's life for one's friends" (John 15:13). Perhaps the best proof of God's love for us is that "while we were still sinners Christ died for us" (Romans 5:8). Hence the burden is not on God to prove his interest in us; the burden is on us to believe in a truth that has already been proven in no uncertain way. This truth is very important for us to believe when it comes to prayer. It should help us to relax and gently make known our needs to God, trusting in his interest just as we would trust in the interest of a good friend.

Realization of our primary purpose: A closer relationship with God is the primary purpose of our petitionary prayer. The Garden of Gethsemane was the scene of Jesus' prayer of petition. In Mark 14:36 Jesus asked his Father to preserve his life, to "take this cup away from me"—a very legitimate request. Yet one thing was of greater priority for Jesus—his relationship with his Father. He came to do his Father's will: "Not what I will but what you will" (Mark 14:36).

Behind every prayer of petition—or every prayer, for that matter—should be the fundamental request that our prayer may, above all else, deepen our relationship with God. When we view the prayer of petition in this way, we can say that no prayer goes unanswered. Every prayer of petition should be viewed in the context of our overall relationship with God. The implication is that our prayers of petition ought to be viewed in terms of how they will affect our relationship with God.

For example, if we seek a better salary—a legitimate desire—we should be concerned that extra funds will not diminish our relationship with God or make us less sensitive to the poor. If we pray for an advancement in our careers, we need to keep in mind that in God's design such an advancement may not help our relationship with him or be good for our family life. While it is legitimate to pray to God for what is good in life, we should always see such benefits in the larger context of how they will affect our relationship with God—the greatest good of all. On the spiritual journey the only absolute good is God and his will; all else, even health, is relative to our relationship with him. As we become more mature pray-ers, we should seek and praise God's holy will and submit to it unconditionally. Such an attitude will be our greatest help in dealing with so-called unanswered prayer.

A contrary attitude is found in those who are merely

concerned about obtaining what they want—with little or no concern about how these desires might affect their relationship with God. When people seek physical healing at a healing service, we sometimes see examples of this attitude. They may receive the physical healing, but their spiritual relationship with God remains unchanged. Their main focus is on the gift to be received and not on God, the great giver. There is interest in the giver only insofar as that one has the capacity to give what the seeker wants. To summarize: When we take our requests to God, our overriding concern should be how the granting or the denial of such requests affects our relationship with the Lord.

WHAT TO PRAY FOR

First: We should pray that our primary concern is God and our fidelity to the will of God. All else is relative and it need not be our concern. "Incline my heart according to your will, O Lord" is a prayer that frequently should be on our lips. In praying this prayer of petition, we are asking God to draw our whole being into line with his plan for us.

Second: We should pray that God will help each of us to become the unique and original person we were created to be. Each person is created to be a unique manifestation of God's truth, goodness, and beauty in the world. Our deepest and most authentic fulfillment in life is discovering and becoming that unique person. Here our prayer should be something like this: "Lord, help me to discover and become the self you created me to be, and help me to resist any temptation to try to be a carbon copy of anyone else."

Third: Since all of us have a particular vocation in life (married, religious, single) and a particular career with duties and responsibilities, we certainly should pray frequently that God will help us to be faithful to our particular vocation and duties in life. This means responding to the daily challenges of our life situation in a creative and positive way—and this, despite the temptation to withdraw and say no to the duties and challenges of life.

Fourth: We should pray for our specific needs. Some kind of a "prayer list"—which can be lengthened or shortened at our convenience—can be used on a regular basis. Here is a sample of such a list:

"Father, help me to discover and embrace your will at all times."

"Father, help me to discover and become the person you created me to be."

"Jesus, lead me into a deeper experience of the Father's love for me."

"Jesus, fill my heart with your love for the people you have given me to lead and serve."

"Holy Spirit, help me to use well the gifts of time,
treasure, and talent you have given me."

"Holy Spirit, reveal to me the sin and woundedness that
hinder me from surrendering myself more fully to you."

If this list seems rather self-centered, it is because petitionary prayer is prayer for self as opposed to intercessory prayer,
which is prayer for others.

As the Lord answers very specific prayers, we grow in
our conviction about the value of petitionary prayer. We may
even write down in our spiritual journals the Lord's answers
to special requests. In our prayers of petition we should always
say, "Lord, help me to recognize your answer to my prayer."
Sometimes we are blind to the Lord's answer because we are
locked into wanting God to answer our prayer in a very specific way.

To summarize: It is interesting to note that our requests in
prayer can reveal much about our images of God and self and
our relationship with God. For example, if we don't dare pray
for the seemingly impossible things in life, is it because we
think God can't handle such a request? If we rarely make small
requests such as "Lord, help me to find a parking space," is it
because we have an image of God that causes us to think God
would be too busy to have an interest in our parking problem?
If we rarely pray for ourselves because we think it is selfish,
does this outlook reveal a poor self-image? Do we think we
don't deserve God's attention? If our prayer is primarily dom-

inated by petitionary prayer, what might this say about our relationship with God? If we throw temper tantrums when God doesn't respond to our prayer exactly as we asked, what does this reveal about us and how we relate to God?

THE PROBLEM OF UNANSWERED PRAYER

A very definite cause of alienation from and frustration with God is that we sometimes perceive him as uncaring because he doesn't answer our prayers. This is particularly true when our requests are very close to our heart—such as holding a marriage together, healing a parent of cancer, and similar problems. There does not seem to be a definite or perfect answer to the problem of unanswered prayer, but it is possible to offer some insights on this difficult question.

FOUR REASONS WHY OUR PRAYERS GO UNANSWERED

Obviously there are countless reasons why—from the human viewpoint—our prayers go unanswered. Here, however, are four standard ones to which we can all relate.

We pray with an unforgiving heart. The little boy who prayed, "Forgive us our trash baskets as we forgive those who put their trash in our baskets," had the wrong words but the right idea. When we put our trash in other people's baskets, we not only alienate ourselves from them but also from God who loves them very much. In Mark, Jesus proclaims, "When you stand to pray, forgive anyone against whom you have a grievance" (Mark 11:25). In Matthew, he says, "If you bring your gift to the altar, and there recall that your brother has anything against you, leave your gift there at the altar, go first and be reconciled with your brother, and then come and offer your gift" (Matthew 5:23–24). These sayings of Jesus clearly point out how important it is to go to God with a forgiving heart—or at least with a heart that desires to forgive.

We ask wrongly. "You ask but do not receive, because you ask wrongly" (James 4:3). What are some examples of asking wrongly? We might, for example, pray for a job and not get it. The reason for this is not God but the simple fact that we don't have the skills needed for the job. Again, suppose we ask God to get us through a particular test. We fail the test and get upset with God. The reason we failed, though, was that we didn't study the subject matter sufficiently. When our prayers seem to fall on "deaf ears," we might ask if our action—or lack thereof—caused the problem.

We lack faith and persistence. Deep down we may not really believe that God is interested in our request or that he wants to help us. Or perhaps we ask for something one time and fail to persevere in prayer. St. Monica had to pray many years before her son Augustine turned to God.

We fail to do our part. Failure to do our part is another reason why our prayers go unanswered. We might pray for reconciliation of a particular conflict but be unwilling to admit our own wrong in the relationship. We ask God to bless our worship service, but we do little or nothing to prepare for the service by creating the kind of conditions that facilitate God's action. While God sometimes helps us when we can't help ourselves, he certainly expects us to help ourselves (and others) when possible.

TWO REASONS WHY GOD DOESN'T ALWAYS ANSWER OUR PRAYERS

Besides the four human reasons for unanswered prayer, there are divine reasons for God not answering our prayers. Here are two general reasons that can help us understand our unanswered prayers.

God's ways are not always our ways. In the Book of Isaiah, God tells us, "My thoughts are not your thoughts, nor are your ways my ways" (Isaiah 55:8). In the ebb and flow of our lives, God sometimes "writes straight with crooked lines" or works in strange ways. What might seem to be a no to us might be a yes from God. God may deny our literal request but actually grant us the deeper, perhaps unconscious, desires of our heart. We may have a particular goal we wish to attain, and we may have ideas about how to attain it. God may help us to reach our goal but in ways we never thought of.

Fr. Basil Pennington, in his book *Ways of Prayer*, writes:

God will give us whatever we want, asking in prayer— what we truly want, not what we say we want or even think we want. God listens to the heart, not to the lips. He knows, too, how limited is our understanding and knowledge. He sees our truest desires and knows how they can best be fulfilled. And this is what he grants. We may not see it at the moment, but we will in time. . . . If God seems to be saying "No" to some prayers, it is because he is saying "Yes" to the deepest prayer of our hearts.

When St. Paul asked God to take away his thorn in the flesh, God said no, but only in order that he could say yes to a deeper desire of Paul—namely, to experience the power of God in his being (see 2 Corinthians 12:7–10). A second example of how God sometimes says no to one request of ours so that he can say yes to a deeper request is found in the prayer of a man whose wife was killed in an accident. And although his daughter also died and he himself went blind, he was still able to address God in this magnificent way:

I asked for health,
so that I could do great things for you.
You gave me sickness,
so that I could do greater things.
I asked for riches, so that I could be happy.
You gave me poverty, so that I could be really wise.
I asked for strength, so that I could fight for you.
You gave me weakness, so that I could rely on you.

> I got none of the things I asked for, but all the
> things I hoped for. (Author Unknown)

God's timing differs from our timing. God's timing may not be ours, so we may think that God is refusing our prayer. Eventually, however, we have to admit that God knew best after all.

Many years ago I had a personal experience of the wisdom and giftedness of God's timing in contrast to mine. While residing in another parish, I applied to become pastor of a different parish. Once I had made my formal request, I was anxious, for various reasons, to move as soon as possible. According to the normal way that personnel changes happen in our diocese, I should have been in my new parish by the end of October. In actuality, due to certain circumstances, my appointment was not formalized until the middle of December. I found the waiting period to be very difficult. It was not easy to continue functioning in one place when my mind and emotions were already someplace else.

During these same weeks I was engaged in writing the first draft of this book—a stage of writing that demanded much time and concentration as I tried to collect materials from many different sources. So, while I waited for my new appointment, I had more time than usual to write. As each week went by, I found myself in the paradoxical and humorous position of feeling frustrated with God for not making my transfer happen faster, but also feeling very grateful to him for the time I had to collect resource materials for each new section of the book.

I was particularly grateful when I realized that I would have much less time to write as I became more and more involved in my new parish. If God had moved according to my schedule, I might never have completed this book, or I certainly would not have finished it as soon as I did.

The bottom line in all of this involves growing in the ability to trust in Divine Providence and to trust that God is working out all things for the best (see Romans 8:28). A poem entitled "The Weaver" beautifully sums up all that has been said here about God's ways and our ways:

My life is but a weaving
Between my Lord and me.
I cannot choose the colors
He worketh steadily.
Oft times He weaveth sorrow,
And I in foolish pride
Forget He sees the upper,
And I, the underside.
Not till the loom is silent
And the shuttles cease to fly,
Shall God unroll the canvas
And explain the reason why
The dark threads are as needful
In the Weaver's skillful hand
As the threads of gold and silver
In the pattern He has planned.
(Author Unknown)

Questions for Personal Reflection and Small-Group Discussion

1. What spoke to you most in this chapter?
2. Have you ever had the experience when "God's timing" was better than your own?
3. What helps you to deal with the problem of unanswered prayer?
4. Recall a recent example of God answering your prayer. Was it answered in the exact way you asked?
5. What was your experience with the suggested prayer exercise offered below?

Suggested Prayer Exercise

Draw up for yourself a prayer list—one that expresses the desires of your heart in relationship to God, family, neighbor, self, work, and the larger world.

THREE

Prayer of Intercession

First of all, then, I ask that supplications, prayers, petitions, and thanksgivings be offered for everyone, for kings and for all in authority, that we may lead a quiet and tranquil life in all devotion and dignity. This is good and pleasing to God our savior, who wills everyone to be saved and to come to knowledge of the truth.

1 Timothy 2:1–4

The great men and women of God were great intercessors. Intercession is like a "leaven" in the heart of the Trinity. It is a way of penetrating the Father's heart and discovering new dimensions which can shed light on concrete situations and change them. We can say that God's heart is touched by our intercession, yet in reality he is always there first. What our intercession achieves is that his power, his love and his faithfulness are shown ever more clearly in the midst of the people.

Pope Francis, The Joy of the Gospel, *283*

The prayer of intercession is our prayer for other people and their needs. Sacred Scripture has several stories and images of individuals interceding before God for others. For example, the Book of Exodus relates how Moses frequently interceded before God for his people. A lovely example of this shows Moses pleading with God on behalf of his unfaithful people:

> But Moses implored the Lord, his God, saying, "Why, O Lord, should your wrath blaze up against your own people, whom you brought out of the land of Egypt with such great power and with so strong a hand? Why should the Egyptians say, 'With evil intent he brought them out, that he might kill them in the mountains and exterminate them from the face of the earth'? Let your blazing wrath die down; relent in punishing your people. Remember your servants Abraham, Isaac and Israel, and how you swore to them by your own self, saying, 'I will make your descendants as numerous as the stars in the sky; and all this land that I promised, I will give your descendants as their perpetual heritage.'" So the Lord relented in the punishment he had threatened to inflict on his people. (Exodus 32:11–14)

There are also many examples of intercessory prayers in the New Testament. In the Cana story, we see Mary interceding for a young couple (see John 2:1–12). In Matthew 8:5–13, the Roman centurion intercedes with Jesus on behalf of his sick servant. In Luke 19:41–44, Jesus weeps over Jerusalem, crying out for her conversion.

Through this type of prayer, we, in a spirit of solidarity, enter into the pain of others and go before the throne of God on their behalf. Basil Pennington, in *Ways of Prayer*, writes: "Intercessory prayer is not a question of a lot of prayers; it is a question of a lot of love. He or she who loves much accomplishes much when that love is coupled with strong faith."

By means of intercessory prayer we join with Jesus who "lives forever" to intercede for all who come to God through him (see Hebrews 7:25). As baptized persons sharing in the priesthood of Christ, we are all called to join Jesus' ministry of intercession. In the spirit of Mary at Cana, we bring the hurts, the pain, and the needs of our brothers and sisters to Jesus, trusting, like Mary, that he will do something.

Many years ago I had the opportunity to spend a few days at Bethany House of Intercession in Providence, Rhode Island, a house of prayer (no longer in existence) run by a group of priests whose main ministry was to intercede continuously for priests throughout the world. Priests from all over the world visited this house of prayer. Each time a newcomer arrived, the group would gather around him and pray that God would grant him the gifts of intercession, listening, and compassion.

Even though many of the priests who came to Bethany House were heavily burdened with personal problems, they were asked upon entry to focus on the burdens of others rather than on their own burdens, trusting that as they reached out in compassion to others, God would take care of their needs. Invariably they all found that while being concerned with the needs of others, God quietly took care of their needs.

All were asked to pray specifically for priests with problems and struggles similar to their own (discouragement, depression, worry, alcoholism, anger, or whatever). After several days of praying for a priest with a problem similar to their own, most of them received the healing they needed. The priests discovered that their own wounds were touched and healed as they learned, through intercessory prayer, how much Jesus loved another person who was just like them. Those who devote themselves to the ministry of healing know this quite well. Some say that the easiest way to receive a healing is to pray for someone similar to ourselves and pray with deep compassion for them.

WAYS OF INTERCEDING

What are some forms of intercession or ways to intercede for other people? The prayer list to which I referred earlier also contains a list of names and concerns that I wish to bring before the Lord in intercession. Usually I just go through the list, mentioning each person or concern and asking God to take care of the situation. Sometimes I'll use the Rosary as a way to pray.

Matthew Linn, who also wrote *Prayer Course in Healing Life's Hurts,* has several suggestions for intercessory prayer:

Choose something you often struggle with (for example, envy, anxiety, some physical ailment, or other difficulty) and intercede for someone with a similar struggle.

Read the newspaper and intercede for one person whose difficulties are recorded there.

Stand in the place of another and receive the Eucharist for him or her.

Like the centurion in Luke 7:1-10, bring someone to Jesus and ask for healing. Try to see that person with the eyes of Jesus and strive to feel Jesus' compassion for him or her. Once you are filled with the compassion of Jesus, see yourself laying your hand upon that person and see that person filled with light and strength as you breathe Jesus' life into him or her.

One elderly lady says she has a big bushel basket, and when people ask for prayers, she just "throws their petitions into the bushel basket," trusting that God will take care of them.

Intercession can also be done in a group. For example, some couples gather together to pray for God's blessing, strength, and protection on their marriages. Others gather to pray for the spiritual renewal of the parish and for people who are struggling in any way.

As with the prayer of petition, we have no guarantee that our prayers of intercession will be answered exactly as we want. Not everyone Jesus prayed for was changed. "He was not able to perform any mighty deed there [his own part of the country], apart from curing a few sick people by laying his hands on them. He was amazed at their lack of faith" (Mark 6:5–6). While we can't guarantee that the people we pray for will be changed, we can be sure that *we* will be changed.

Questions for Personal Reflection and Small-Group Discussion

1. What spoke to you most in this chapter?
2. Which of the suggestions for intercessory prayer in this chapter appeal to you most?
3. "The easiest way to receive healing is to pray for someone who is just like us and to pray with the deep compassion of Jesus." What are your thoughts on this suggestion?
4. What was your experience with the suggested prayer exercise offered below?

Suggested Prayer Exercise

Choose something you often struggle with and begin to intercede for someone with a similar struggle. This is most beneficial if you have a specific person in mind.

FOUR

Prayer of Contrition

*If we say, "We are without sin," we deceive ourselves,
and the truth is not in us. If we acknowledge our
sins, he is faithful and just and will forgive our
sins and cleanse us from every wrongdoing.*

1 John 1:8–9

*We must be sorry for our sinfulness. Sorrow is the
fruit of love. When we realize God's overwhelming
love for us in spite of our past refusal to accept
his love, how can we help but respond in love?*

David E. Rosage

St. John's words quoted above assure us not only of the reality of sin but also of the reality of God's mercy. To be careless or unconcerned about sin is to be careless and unconcerned about what separates us from God and others. Refusing to recognize and deal with the presence of sin in our spiritual lives is like refusing to recognize and deal with the presence of some ailment in our physical lives. Likewise, ignoring the prayer of contrition is ignoring the divine medicine God provides to purify us of sin.

WHAT IS SIN?

Sin is a mysterious, ugly reality that can be described in count-less ways.

Sin not only separates us from God and others, it also sep-arates us from self and creation.

Sin allows our false selves to dominate our attitudes, words, and behavior.

Sin is primarily an attitude of the heart. Some people move through the day and, technically speaking, commit no sins; yet their whole attitude is sinful because they have lived their day in disregard of relationship, keeping God and people at a cool, unloving distance.

Sin is the prodigal son leaving his father's house and want-ing to live his life while refusing to relate with his father (see Luke 15:11–13). Cut off from his father's love, the son starts to disintegrate, even to the point of eating with the swine. He loses all self-respect. When we sin we place ourselves in a state of alienation and disintegration and in need of resto-ration and healing.

Sin is usually a manifestation of weakness; only rarely does it manifest malice. Most of us want to serve and love God, and we very rarely shut God out of our lives deliberately. Frequently through weakness and lack of priorities, however, we forget about God or allow other more tangible objects and people to take his place. When Peter denied that he knew Jesus, he sinned through human weakness. Frightened for his life, he became a coward and a weakling.

WHY WE NEED CONTRITION

If sin is the cancer that destroys our peace and our relationship with God, contrition is the healing medicine that God provides to restore our peace and our relationship with him. It is faith in God's merciful love, our desire to be at peace with him, and our desire to grow in our relationship with the Lord that move us to go to God in sorrow for our sins. To the extent that we do not believe in God's mercy or desire his peace and reconciliation, to that extent we will not be very interested in praying the prayer of contrition.

"What exactly is contrition?" we may ask. Contrition is a gift that God places in our hearts to help us to see the ugliness and destructiveness of sin and to turn away from it and seek God. In his state of sin and alienation from God, the prodigal son said: "I shall get up and go to my father and I shall say to him, 'Father, I have sinned against heaven and against you. I no longer deserve to be called your son'" (Luke 15:18). So contrition is a *turning away from sin* (that which destroys life) and a *turning toward God* (the One who offers us life). Without the gift of a contrite heart, we are blind to or unaware of the ugliness of sin; we have no desire to turn away from sin and return to God our Father.

HOW TO BECOME CONTRITE

First: We should frequently pray for a contrite heart—for a heart that recognizes the destructiveness of sin, that is repentant of sin, and that once again seeks intimacy with God. Here is a suggested prayer: "Jesus, help me to see the sins (the attitudes and behaviors) in my life that block my growth in you and that hinder me from being a more loving person." Often, like King David, we are blind to the sin in our lives (see 2 Samuel 12:1–6). Also, we could use Psalm 51 (David's prayer of repentance) to pray for a contrite heart.

Second: We should pray for the grace to overcome some sinful attitude or behavior in our lives. For example, we may suffer from a critical spirit. A suggested prayer in that situation is the following: "Lord, help me to see why I tend to be so critical of others and myself. Also, Lord, grant me the grace I need to keep struggling to overcome this destructive behavior. Or better still, why don't you just rid my heart of all desire to criticize others and myself in a destructive way." Of course, we may have to pray that prayer for months or years, or even a lifetime.

Third: We should pray that we feel and accept the mercy that God offers to each one of us. "Lord, help me to believe that you truly have forgiven my sins. Help me to believe that you hold no record of my past failures" (see 2 Corinthians 13:5–6). When we cannot forgive ourselves, often the problem is pride and a strong perfectionist trait in our personalities. Here we need to remember that our great need to be perfect is not a major concern for God. God knows well that if he allowed us to become perfect, we might quickly forget our need for him.

St. Paul came to realize this when he reflected on his

thorn-in-the-flesh experience. By not removing the thorn, God kept Paul in a state of humble dependence. Paul eventually saw God's wisdom and even rejoiced in it. "I will rather boast most gladly of my weaknesses, in order that the power of Christ may dwell with me" (2 Corinthians 12:9).

Fourth: We should thank God for the gift of unceasing mercy. We can even thank God for our sins—the sins that lead us to experience his mercy, the sins that hopefully lead us to have compassion for other people in their weakness. People who think they are sinless tend to be very judgmental of others. Our sins keep us humble, dependent on God, and in need of mercy. Of course, we should always struggle to eradicate sin because sin damages our lives and destroys the harmony of God's beautiful creation (see Genesis 6:5–7).

Fifth: We should pray for true contrition. We Catholic Christians believe that sin not only diminishes our relationship with Christ but also with the members of his Body, the Church. Therefore, reconciliation of sin must include not only restoring our friendship with Christ but also with our own community of believers. In the sacrament of penance (reconciliation), the priest represents not only Christ but also his Body, the Church: "Whose sins you shall forgive, they are forgiven them." In the confessional, the priest is a visible, tangible sign of God's healing mercy. At this particular time and place, we hear Jesus in an audible, human way say to us, "Go in peace; your sins are forgiven." What could be more comforting, reassuring, and healing?

Questions for Personal Reflection and Small-Group Discussion

1. What spoke to you most in this chapter?
2. "God wants to use our sins and weaknesses to bring us closer to him. The devil wants to use them to discourage us and drive us away from God." What are your thoughts on this statement?
3. What sin(s) do you find hard to forgive in others or in yourself?
4. What was your experience with the suggested prayer exercise offered below?

Suggested Prayer Exercise

Spend some time calling to mind a past sin or failure for which you still feel unreconciled or unhealed. Then imagine Jesus being present with you. Speak with him (in word or in writing) about your failure and hurt. Then tell him you are sorry and ask him for his forgiveness and healing. Finally, imagine Jesus embracing you and restoring to you his peace and reconciliation.

FIVE

The Prayer of Forgiveness

When you stand to pray, forgive anyone against whom you have a grievance, so that your heavenly Father may in turn forgive you your transgressions.

MARK 11:25

Asking for forgiveness is the prerequisite for both the Eucharistic liturgy and personal prayer.

CATECHISM OF THE CATHOLIC CHURCH, 2631

"Let each one of you think about a person with whom you do not get along, with whom you are angry. In silence, think about this person, pray for this person and let yourself become merciful towards this person."

POPE FRANCIS

Nothing is clearer in the Gospel than Jesus' command to forgive life's hurts, and nothing can be more difficult.

In the lives of families, parents sometimes miserably fail and hurt their children. Children sometimes do terrible things to their parents. Siblings hurt each other so much that they to go their graves unreconciled. In parish families, parishioners sometimes offend and fail each other. Sadly, some of our priests and even bishops have ended up in prison for hurting children. Many institutions commit grave injustices against their employees. As we can see, forgiveness can be one of the most difficult things that any Christian can be called to do.

When it seems that forgiveness of some hurts and crimes is impossible, we do well to look at inspiring examples of forgiveness in our world. Who will ever forget the words of forgiveness spoken by parishioners of Mother Emmanuel Church in Charleston to the young man who had slaughtered their pastor and eight other parishioners?

When the Truth and Reconciliation Commission was set up in South Africa to heal the hurts of decades of apartheid and human abuses, an American couple, Peter and Linda Biehl, went to South Africa to meet and embrace the people who killed their twenty-six-year-old daughter.

These are just two examples that show how forgiveness is always possible for those who really want to act on this piece of the Gospel.

DEFINING FORGIVENESS—
WHAT IT IS AND ISN'T

Forgiveness doesn't mean condoning, minimizing, or excusing a hurt done to us. It doesn't mean surrendering a right to justice when, for example, someone has stolen from us. Forgiveness is a decision to let go of a hurt done to us. It is the gift we give ourselves so we do not allow the hurt to control our emotions. In the words of Jean Maalouf, "Forgiveness is the powerful assertion that bad things will not ruin your today even though they may have spoiled your past." We know that forgiveness is occurring when the distance between our offender and us is peaceful and not hostile. Before we look at how prayer can help us to let go of a hurt, here are ten common obstacles to letting go of a particular hurt.

TEN OBSTACLES TO
FORGIVING LIFE'S HURTS

Obstacle # 1. We may have little or no practice at forgiveness or we may have the tendency to ignore hurts.
Obstacle #2. We may feel strongly that our offender does not deserve to be forgiven. If we feel this way, do we deserve God's mercy or the mercy of those we have offended?
Obstacle #3. Intellectually, we may feel consciously—or more likely unconsciously—that Jesus' stand on forgiveness is wrong. In truth, we may feel that some offenses are unforgivable.

Obstacle #4. Pride and a hardened heart are common blocks to forgiveness.

Obstacle #5. Forgiving a hurt may seem like *minimizing* or *excusing* the hurt.

Obstacle #6. Forgiveness involves dealing with emotions that most of us do not like to face, such as anger, hatred, and a need for revenge.

Obstacle #7. We may fear that forgiveness would leave us vulnerable to being hurt again.

Obstacle #8. We do not want to talk to God about the hurt because we so strongly resist letting go of it.

Obstacle #9. We may not be able to get beyond the anger and rage connected to the hurt.

Obstacle #10. We may be so deep in the "righteous victim" stance that we are unable or have no desire to move out of it.

THREE PRAYER SUGGESTIONS

The following are three suggestions on how to use prayer to move from a deep hurt in our lives to a place of forgiveness.

Suggestion #1. Praying for a desire to forgive. When someone has hurt us deeply, we may have little or no desire to forgive. Rather, we may be so angry that we are consumed with getting even. When we feel this way, we may want to use the following prayer or one like it.

Jesus, you know how much I despise N_____ and how I have absolutely no desire to forgive him. In fact, my only desire is to get even with him/her. Yet, I also know that continuing to rage against this person is no good for my body, mind, or spirit and is certainly contrary to your word which calls us to forgive life's hurts. So I humbly ask you to do for me what I cannot do for myself. Place in my heart a desire to forgive this person for the sake of my own well-being and for the sake of my relationship with you.

We may have to say that prayer fervently *many* times before we notice any desire to work through our hurt and anger. Just as physical therapy takes time, so it is with *spiritual* therapy. We have to stretch ourselves a lot emotionally and spiritually if we want God to melt a heart that is hardened. This may be the toughest step in the entire process. Many people choose not to even pray for the desire to forgive.

Suggestion #2. Prayer of repentance. When a hurt occurs, it is rare that we are *totally* free of all wrongdoing. We may be guilty of talking about our offender in an un-Christian way. This step in the forgiveness process is very important because it calls us to stop focusing on the sin of our offender and to start owning *our own* sin. A helpful prayer at this stage may be the following:

Jesus, as you know, I have no problem focusing on the wrong that N_____ has done to me, but I am reluctant to admit the wrong I may have done before, during, or after this

hurt occurred. Please help me to have the courage to name my
wrongdoing and forgive me for my sins in this relationship.

Suggestion #3. Prayer for the offender. I have personally found
that the decision to begin to pray for an offender can be very
helpful in the forgiveness process. It is always helpful to keep
in mind that people hurt us or fail us not because they are evil
monsters, but because they, like us, are imperfect, wounded,
and sinful people. Just as we often need God's mercy and the
mercy of others, we need to be ready, with God's grace, to
share his mercy with others. A helpful prayer at this time may
be the following:

Lord, you created N_____ wonderfully just as you created
me. You love this person just as you love me—with all my
faults and weaknesses. You know I don't love this person very
much at this time, but you do. Share with me your love for
him/her. Also, God, I ask you to bless this scoundrel. Some-
times I, too, am a scoundrel and in need of your blessing.

If we fervently say these prayers over and over, we will most
likely discover that God is creating a new heart in us.

FORGIVING ONESELF

Sometimes, we may believe God and our offenders have forgiven us, but we cannot forgive ourselves. How can prayer

help us to forgive ourselves?

If we have committed a grave sin, we need to seek the grace of true contrition and to go to the sacrament of reconciliation. When someone has confessed a grave sin such as an abortion, an extramarital affair, or a serious act of injustice, and still feels a lot of guilt, I often say: "Satan will want you to continue feeling very bad about this sin. If and when you experience a 'guilt attack,' pray: 'Jesus, you know I am truly sorry for this sin. I believe you have forgiven me, and I accept your mercy. Now, Satan, get out of here!'"

When we have a difficult time forgiving ourselves, it is good to remember that, because of our childhood formation, we may carry within us a perfectionistic spirit which is ready to pounce on us whenever we do wrong. In this case, we may have to learn to talk back to our *inner critic*. (For information on the topic of forgiveness, see my book *How to Forgive Yourself and Others*, pubished by Liguori).

Questions for Personal Reflection and Small-Group Discussion

1. What spoke to you most in this chapter?
2. What obstacles do you face when it comes to forgiving life's hurts?
3. If you believe you have become a more forgiving person, what has contributed to this growth?
4. What advice would you give to someone struggling to forgive a big hurt?
5. What was your experience with the suggested prayer exercise offered below?

Suggested Prayer Exercise

Identify a hurt or grievance that you cling to and that you haven't let go of yet. Then pray about it for a period of time, using the suggestions offered in this chapter.

SIX

Prayer of Consciousness Examen

Mary kept all these things, reflecting
on them in her heart.

LUKE 2:19

To some extent, each of us tends to live in a
state of wakeful sleep, more or less consciously
going through the motions of our everyday life
and experience. Rarely do we take time to get
in touch with and to reflect upon the deeper
meanings of our experiences. We tend to think
that such reflection is simply a waste of time.

CLAIRE BRISSETTE

The key challenge of the spiritual life is to lead a life that is in tune with the Holy Spirit so we can be guided along the path God created for us. St. John says, "Whoever has ears ought to hear what the Spirit says to the churches" (Revelation 2:7). Insofar as we do not have sensitive spiritual ears to hear the words of the Spirit, we run the risk of traveling in all directions, led not by the Holy Spirit but by inner, uncontrolled impulses and outer, passing fads. Like Martha we may become busy doing many good things but miss out on what the Lord is telling us (see Luke 10:38–42). Or, like the Israelites, we may spend many years traveling a part of the spiritual journey that we could have traveled in a much shorter time if we had learned to listen and respond to the promptings of the Holy Spirit. We can say that a key aspect of spiritual growth is learning to become a spirit-listener.

One of the best spiritual exercises we have available to help us to become spirit-listeners is the Consciousness Examen. The Consciousness Examen is a spiritual exercise popularized by St. Ignatius of Loyola. It is said that St. Ignatius used to tell his novices that if they had to omit all the spiritual exercises of the day but one, he would want them to be faithful to the Consciousness Examen.

The main purpose of this spiritual exercise is not to tally up the failures or successes of the day, as we often do in the traditional examination of conscience, but to help us to grow in our sensitivity and responsiveness to the voice of the Holy Spirit. The exercise helps us to see how attentive and responsive we were to the Holy Spirit in the encounters and events of a given day. It also helps us to become conscious of how our sinful side may be luring us away from the Father's loving call and leading us to live a life according to the flesh. Lastly, it helps us to integrate prayer and the activities of our day.

While some writers identify five steps in the Consciousness Examen, this exercise will be divided into three steps, with the third step including the other two steps.

THREE STEPS IN THE EXAMEN PROCESS

Step One: Pray to the Holy Spirit for guidance and courage. We begin by taking a minute or two to quiet down and become aware of God's loving presence. We know in faith—even if we can't feel it—that God loves us unconditionally. When we know we are loved in this manner, we usually find it easier to look at the less attractive sides of our personality. This demands courage on our part. This is why it is important to ask the Holy Spirit to help us face our true selves. Having relaxed and entered into the presence of God, we then pray to the Holy Spirit for guidance and courage.

The following prayer is most appropriate:

Holy Spirit, help me to see the encounters and events of this day as you would want me to see them. Since I cannot focus on or look at everything, help me to reflect on the encounters or events that you would want me to consider. Also give me the courage to face my inner demons, the attitudes and behaviors on which I'd prefer not to reflect.

Step Two: As led by the Spirit, reflect on a particular event or encounter. Having prayed to the Spirit, we should take a minute or two to allow the events and encounters of the day to come before our mental television screen and then decide on an event or encounter on which to focus. When we decide on a particular event or encounter, we should try to see and be in touch with what was happening in that event. What were our attitudes and behavior like? Were we being true to ourselves or acting like frauds? Here we may look back and see that God was inviting us to listen to someone but we decided to turn that person off and center on our own preoccupations. Perhaps we felt the Spirit prompting us to offer a word of encouragement or affirmation, to seek forgiveness, but we decided to be silent and distant.

Another way to look at the day is to ask:
- To what extent was my day Christ-centered, other-centered, or self-centered?
- When I got up in the morning and moved through the day, what attitudes or behaviors dominated? Was I loving, caring, aggressive, or short-tempered?
- Did I try to meet people and events in a Christlike way, or was I basically concerned only about myself and my projects?
- To what extent did I reverence Christ in the people I met? Did I treat people in a utilitarian way, basing my response to them on the basis of their usefulness to me and my projects?

Such reflection should help us grow in self-knowledge and help us to be more aware of the attitudes and behaviors that dominate the flow of our days.

Step Three: Offer prayers of thanks, repentance, healing, and petition. Having reflected on some event(s) or encounter(s) of the day, we can now spend a few minutes talking to the Lord about our good and not-so-good responses. Such a conversation changes what might be a self-centered, introspective reflection into a God-centered one.

For the blessings of the day we give thanks. We also should give thanks for the times we manifested caring attitudes and behaviors, for the times we recognized the Spirit's promptings and responded positively.

For the negative and unloving attitudes and behaviors, for the times we did not respond as the Lord was asking us to respond, we seek God's forgiveness. For negative attitudes and behaviors that reveal not so much our sinfulness but our woundedness and tiredness, we ask for God's healing and strength.

For the help, strength, and courage we need to continue our desire to hear God's voice and our efforts to do his will in all things, we can offer prayers of petition. We also can ask God's blessing on the people we met that day, especially those who were hurting or whom we may have hurt in some way.

Ideally we should set aside a quiet time each evening for the Consciousness Examen, but we may often have to settle for less than the ideal. Therefore we may find ourselves doing this spiritual exercise on our way home from work, when jogging, when in the shower, as a family at dinner, or as we lie down to sleep at night.

What is important here is not so much when and how we make a Consciousness Examen but that we actually take time for this prayer activity. Without regular periods of reflective silence in the presence of God, we will fail to grow in self-knowledge; we will be out of touch with our feelings and inner urgings; and, worst of all, we will become people who are driven and controlled by our excessive needs, desires, compulsions, and inordinate attachments. The noisy crowd and not the noiseless Spirit will become our guide.

Questions for Personal Reflection and Small-Group Discussion

1. What spoke to you most in this chapter?
2. "Insofar as we do not develop an inner spiritual ear, we will run the risk of traveling in all directions, not led by the Spirit of God but by inner, uncontrolled impulses and outer, passing fads." What are your thoughts about this statement?
3. Can you see a difference between the way you respond to life when you live reflectively and when you live unreflectively? If so, describe these differences.
4. What was your experience with the suggested prayer exercise offered below?

Suggested Prayer Exercise

Several times this week, take ten minutes (preferably toward the end of the day) to pray reflectively in the manner outlined in this chapter.

SEVEN

Praying with a Spiritual Journal

Take a scroll and write on it all the
words I have spoken to you.

JEREMIAH 36:2

Journal keeping clearly ... has a past and present
tradition in the Church as a valued way of growing in
the likeness of Christ and a helpful method of praying.

JOSEPH M. CHAMPLIN

Journals serve different purposes for different people. Some people keep them just to log the events of daily life. For others, journal-keeping can be a form of therapy. St. Augustine used writing to unburden his conscience. Emerson said that no matter how disheveled the day, all disasters seem less painful in the evening once they are recorded. When Dag Hammarskjold began keeping a journal, he called it "a sort of white book concerning my negotiations with myself and with God."

Journaling helps us to place the days and years of our lives in proper perspective. Judged by the days—each one viewed individually—life does not make sense. Judged by the years, however, it does add up, and a plan emerges. Professor Ed Fischer (in an article appearing in the *Notre Dame Magazine*) writes:

> A good reason to write a memoir is to have the satisfaction, the consolation of seeing a pattern form. . . . A journal can help you find a pattern in your life, a theme, a recurring motif. . . . It will help you get a glimpse of what you are becoming. Rereading a journal is like coming upon a wall where in youth you stood from time to time to chalk your height, or like paging through an old family album. How you changed and you didn't even notice!

The reflections of Professor Fischer should help us to see how journal-keeping in general can serve many useful and wonderful purposes. The purpose of a *spiritual* journal, however, is more specific and focused. Its primary aim is to help us live our lives more in tune with the Spirit of God, to help us detect the thread of God's weaving in our daily lives. In a spiritual journal we try to identify the leadings of the Spirit in our lives and record how we are responding or not responding to such leadings. We search for what helps or hinders us from hearing and responding to the Spirit in our daily events and encounters. As we discipline ourselves to write in our journals and reread our entries periodically, we will be able to detect trends and patterns—where we are coming from and where we are going in life.

A spiritual journal is an excellent tool to help us slow down in a fast-moving world and develop a reflective attitude toward life. It is a way to identify and record the moods, voices, fantasies, daydreams, anxieties, and blessings of a given day—a way to name, vent, and defuse the tough feelings of life and try to see all these in terms of our relationship with God. Using a spiritual journal gives us a chance to meet the Lord in a new way, to personalize our faith, and to learn the difference between our stated and lived values. If we work with a spiritual director, a spiritual journal can help us to remember what has been going on in our life since our previous meeting.

Some people use a spiritual journal to write "letters to God." Henri Nouwen's book, *A Cry for Mercy: Prayers from the Genesee*, is an excellent example of such letter writing to God. This book gives an inside view of the spiritual life of one of the world's most popular writers and speakers. In this book he offers a "soul-teaching" on prayer.

THE IMPORTANCE OF HONESTY

Honesty is a very important part of journal-keeping. What probably inhibits our honesty most is the fear of someone reading what we have written down. Consequently we tend to write only what we want "posterity" to know about us. We should, of course, do all that we can to resist the temptations of the false self that tells us to write only the nice things.

To help protect the privacy of my journal, I always write on the inside cover, "Private Journal: Please Do Not Read." I conceal personal names by using initials or even by creating nicknames. Some kind of shorthand or code-word system could also be used, and the journal could be kept under lock and key. For me the fear of someone reading my journal has diminished. I have been greatly helped in letting go of this fear by my belief that what is most personally and intimately felt is also most universally felt. If people are scandalized by my wilder thoughts, fantasies, and feelings, it is only because they are out of touch with the evil or shadowy side of their own personalities.

FOUR SUGGESTIONS FOR
JOURNAL WRITING

What is a good way to keep a journal? In answer to that question, here are some suggestions that should prove helpful.

First suggestion: Come to a place of quiet. (This could even be a bench in the center of a shopping mall or a seat on an airplane or train.) Anyway, begin by quieting down within. We can then become aware of God's love and ask his Spirit to help us become aware of what is going on within us right now or during the past few hours or days.

Then we can ask: "What do I find myself daydreaming about? What thoughts are on my mind when I wake up in the middle of the night or in the morning? What are my pressing concerns right now?" As we become aware of what is going on within us, we can begin to jot it down. It is very important to avoid at this point any moralizing on what is flowing out from within. We should put all judgment aside, at least temporarily, and simply allow ourselves to freely express our spontaneous thoughts and feelings. There is no need to analyze or dissect our experiences. Just "be there" with them and see what they might be telling us about our inner selves.

In order to do this, we will often have to tell our inner voices (such as our ideal self or intellectual self) to be quiet. As we write, or after we have finished, we should invite Jesus to be a part of the process. We can tell him how we feel about what we have written. Then we should pause and try to become aware of what we think Jesus would say to us in response. This may be difficult initially or seem to be contrived. But the fact is that the Spirit of Jesus lives within us, and we can assume that he would want to say something to us about the stuff going on in our lives. It would be very good to share with a spiritual director the words we place in Jesus' mouth, because these words would very much reflect our image of God, which may or may not be very distorted.

Second suggestion: Use the journal to get in touch with a troublesome mood that may be "possessing" us at any given moment of the day. Until such a mood or "demon" is named and rebuked, it will have power over us and be an obstacle to our efforts to live our day in a Christlike manner. (For a good perspective on bad moods and the spiritual life, consult chapter three of *Moving in the Spirit*, by Richard Hauser, SJ.)

Third suggestion: Use the journal to express and deal with tough feelings which may have arisen because of some issue or encounter. It is good to journal about any anxiety or insecurity we are feeling within ourselves, or about angry or jealous feelings. When the feelings we have within are related to some relationship or some encounter we've had with another person, we may find it useful to imagine that person sitting down in front of us.

At this point I personally use the journal to "speak my mind" and say my bit, grateful that I cannot be interrupted or do not have to be worried about what I say. Martin Luther found that to rage against his enemies helped him to pray better. A journal is a good place to rage. If the released rage leaves more space in the heart for prayer, that alone is a good reason for keeping a journal.

In both of the above situations (dealing with troublesome moods or with tough feelings), we should invite Jesus to be a part of what is going on. We could say, "Jesus, this is what is going on with me; please help me with it." Then we should pause and become one with our moods as we give them to Jesus. We can imagine him looking at us with eyes of love and concern. Then we can invite his response with the words, "Speak, Lord, your servant is listening." Often we may be afraid to face what is within us and be scared to bring it to Jesus, unsure of how he may react. But if we can't face and befriend the "enemy" within, how can we expect to face and befriend the enemies outside of us?

Fourth suggestion: Use the spiritual journal to identify some helps and hindrances in our lives as we try to live in the Spirit. Journaling can help us as we attempt to become more flexible clay in the hands of God whose great plan is to reshape us in the image and likeness of Jesus.

These four suggestions should help those who wish to use a spiritual journal as part of their prayer life. People who feel drawn to this way of praying—spiritual journaling is not for everyone—could search out other resources that give many practical suggestions on how to make the spiritual journal a valuable means of spiritual growth.

Questions for Personal Reflection and Small-Group Discussion

1. What spoke to you most in this chapter?
2. In what ways do you think spiritual journaling could aid you in your prayer life?
3. Have you ever kept a journal, a spiritual one or some other kind? If so, what was that experience like for you?
4. What was your experience with the suggested prayer exercise offered below?

Suggested Prayer Exercise

Take ten to fifteen minutes to journal about your own death. Ask yourself: What would you find most difficult about dying? What would you fear most? What would you want to say to your friends before you die? What would you want to be remembered for? What words would you want on your tombstone?

EIGHT

Decisioning Prayer

Choose life, then, that you and your
descendants may live, by loving the Lord,
your God, heeding his voice, and holding fast
to him. For that will mean life for you.

DEUTERONOMY 30:19–20

Since the mysterious voice of the Spirit is not the
only voice we hear but comes to us accompanied
by the tumultuous sounds of our own conflicting
impulses and the clamoring of the entire creation, it
is essential for us to be able to discern the presence
of the Spirit in order to choose to say "yes" to him.

THOMAS GREEN, SJ

"Should I marry John?"

"Should I get out of or stay in this unhappy marriage?"

"Should I quit my present career and take up something less lucrative but more fulfilling?"

"Should I join or quit a particular ministry in my parish or community?"

Decisions, decisions, decisions. . . . Life is full of them, big and small, and sometimes it seems so difficult to know exactly what God is asking of us. When it comes to decision-making, many of us would like very much to dial Heaven 27 and say, as I do: "Hi, Lord, this is your friend Eamon. I am faced with this particular decision, and I was wondering which way I ought to go. Could you please let me know as soon as possible. Thanks." Even though no such direct line to God exists, that is not to say that no divine guidance is available to us. As Christians we believe that because the Holy Spirit lives in our hearts (see 1 Corinthians 6:19) we can indeed come to a good sense of his truth for our lives.

Before he left this world to return to his Father, Jesus promised us the gift of his Spirit. He told his disciples, "I will ask the Father, and he will give you another Advocate to be with you always, the Spirit of truth" (John 14:16–17). A central activity of the Holy Spirit in our lives is to lead us into the truth by helping us to discover and walk God's path for our lives. Because the Holy Spirit is not the only voice that seeks to guide us in life, we Christians need help when it comes to decision-making. Besides the voice of God, there are many other voices that call out to us, seeking to attract us and influence us to walk in a particular direction.

Even a quick reading of modern-day literature on Christian decision-making (often called discernment) helps us to see that the decision-making process can be a rather complex process, basically due to our lack of self-knowledge, our lack of inner freedom, and our great ability to try to have God say "yes" to what we ourselves want. Yet none of this should discourage us. With the Holy Spirit on our side and a willingness to learn—through reading, through dialoguing with other mature Christians, and especially through the trial-and-error method—we will be pleasantly surprised at how quickly we can grow in our ability to recognize and discern the voice of God from voices that are not of the Lord. One of the best spiritual exercises available to help us to grow in the art of Christian decision-making is the Prayer of Consciousness Examen outlined in chapter six.

Are there any practical ways available to help us discover God's will in a specific situation? There are no foolproof ways that will lead us to absolute certainty concerning God's will in a particular situation, but there are specific guidelines that can help us to grow in our ability to perceive and discern God's call and action in our lives. These steps could be called: "A Beginner's Guide to Christian Decision-Making." As we grow in the art and gift of discernment, we will develop a method that best works for us.

Here are seven steps that should help bring our prayer life into our decision-making process.

SEVEN STEPS TO DISCERNMENT

First Step: Formulate a proposition. Start by making a clear statement or question of what we are trying to decide. For example: "Should I change careers?" "Should I terminate my relationship with so-and-so?" "Should I join a particular ministry in my parish?"

Second Step: Gather the relevant data. Write down the various alternatives available and consider the advantages and disadvantages of each. Take into consideration the effect each alternative would have on our relationship with God, our family, or any other individual(s) or group(s). As we end this step, we need to identify the alternative or option that we feel most drawn toward or the option to which we feel most attached.

Third Step: Bring the gathered data to prayer. This is the heart of the discernment process. It involves praying about the available options before the Lord with the purpose of seeing which option gives us the greatest sense of God's peace. As we pray, it is important for us to see if there is one option that we feel we want more than the others. If there is, then we need to ask: "How willing am I to let go of that option if it seems God is calling me in another direction?" In other words, how free and willing are we to embrace any option that the Lord might offer? Often we are so attached to a particular direction that we are not free to move in another direction—hence, the vital importance of praying for the grace of inner freedom.

We are at the point of *inner freedom* when we are detached enough from every available option to freely walk down any path the Lord may call us to walk. Sometimes it may take weeks or even months to come to that point of detachment or inner freedom. Ideally we should not choose a *particular* option until we are free to embrace every available option.

We need to be aware that where there exists a strong attachment to a particular option, the discernment process is endangered, and our capacity for recognizing God's call is blurred. Of course, in some situations we may never reach the state of complete detachment. That's okay and understandable, but at least we must have a desire for complete detachment and struggle toward that goal.

Personally I find this part of the discernment process to be the most important and the most challenging. It is not easy to say in all sincerity: "Thy kingdom come, not mine. Thy will be done, not mine." Of course, with God's grace all things are possible.

As we engage in the struggle to embrace God's will, it is important for us to know that our deepest and truest self desires God's will. It is our false, sinful, and unredeemed self that resists God's will. But it is God's will which leads us to true freedom and true happiness. The voice in us that does not believe this is the voice of the false self, not the true self.

As we pray about the various options available, we need to distinguish between what we think and feel when we are in prayer and most open to God's will and what we think and feel outside of prayer when we might be anxious and attached to a particular option. The former is more likely to be God's will for us.

As a part of this third step, St. Ignatius suggests three imaginative exercises. First, we should consider what advice we would give another person faced with the same situation. Second, we can imagine ourselves on our deathbed and ask what we would then wish to have chosen. Third, we can picture ourselves standing before God on the Last Day and consider what decision we would then wish to have made. These exercises help us to distance ourselves from the decision facing us and look at it with some objectivity.

Fourth Step: Make a decision. At some point we must make a decision. We should go with the option that gives us the most peace when we are in prayer. But what if we experience no real peace about the options available to us? In that situation we can either postpone the decision or choose the one least troublesome to us. We should not decide when in doubt; and, if time permits, we should continue to pray until we experience peace about a particular option. Last, we need to be aware that the option chosen may not always be the most attractive one or the one we most desired. Sometimes we may feel led to choose an option with tears—for example, to return to a marriage situation that in the past caused much pain. However, such initial tears of sadness often give way to tears of joy (see 2 Corinthians 7:8–13).

Fifth Step: Live with the decision. Once we come to a decision, it is good to live with it for a while before we actually act on what we decided. This is particularly important if we have a tendency to be impulsive.

Sixth Step: Act on the decision. This may seem obvious, but this step can be the most difficult because it may involve giving up something to which we are still quite attached. We should ask the Holy Spirit to give us the power and courage to act on what we believe to be God's will for our lives.

Seventh Step: Seek confirmation of the decision. Matthew Linn reminds us that the final test for hearing God's will is whether living it out brings life to us and to others. If the choice we make bears good fruit, we can be quite sure we acted in accord with God's will. This is not to say that there won't be struggles connected with our choice nor days when we will wonder, "Did I really make the right choice?" Such struggles and wondering are normal and do not necessarily prove that we made a wrong decision.

But what if we discover later that we did make the wrong decision? Knowing that we made a sincere effort to seek God's will should console us. Discernment is not just a gift but an art learned through trial and error. The Lord doesn't ask that we always be right; God asks only that we always try to be honest and act out of our best understanding of a particular situation. Finally, we can be consoled by remembering God's ability to use our mistakes to his—and our—advantage. God writes straight with crooked lines.

To prepare our hearts for good decision-making, the following prayer by St. Ignatius of Loyola is recommended:

Take, Lord, and receive all my liberty, my memory, my
understanding, and my will, all that I have and possess.
Everything I have is yours, for you have given it all to
me; to you I return it.
Take, Lord, and do what you
like with me,
only give me your grace

and your love,

for that is enough for me.

Amen.

Questions for Personal Reflection and Small-Group Discussion

1. What spoke to you most in this chapter?
2. When faced with a difficult decision, what, if any, particular process do you go through? Do you pray for guidance, or seek the counsel of others?
3. Can you think of a wrong personal decision which God turned to his and your own advantage? Describe what happened.
4. Recall a difficult decision you have had to make. Explain why it was difficult and how you finally reached that decision.
5. What was your experience with the suggested prayer exercise offered below?

Suggested Prayer Exercise

Write down decisions facing you at this time in your life and begin to ask the Holy Spirit to guide you in making them. If the decision needed is an immediate one, use the practical steps offered in this chapter and see how they help you.

NINE

Prayer of Spiritual Reading

*All Scripture is inspired of God and is useful
for teaching, for refutation, for correction,
and for training in righteousness.*

2 TIMOTHY 3:16

*It is a good thing to have a spiritual book to feed your
prayer. What sort of book? It must be a book which
"clicks" with you personally, a book you feel at home
with like a wise and trusted friend, a book which speaks
to your condition. People are always recommending
books to us. "You must read so and so; you must read
such and such." By all means have a look at them, have
a quick browse through, but unless the recommended
book "clicks" with you, forget it. It is not the book for
you now. It may be one day, but not now. We are all
made differently, we all have different needs and we
are all at different stages on the road. Choose your
own book and read it slowly, a little at a time, pausing
to think about it, to chew it over, to take it in.*

EVAN PILKINGTON

The Church has always considered reflective or spiritual reading to be one of the most fundamental exercises of the spiritual life. In and through this meditative type of reading, especially on the Gospels, we come to know the person of Christ and the attitudes and values he embraces. Spiritual reading also nourishes, illumines, and gives direction to our deepest selves, our spirits. Without regular periods of reflective reading, we run the risk of becoming victims of passing fads and allowing ourselves to be led by the wisdom of the world—that wisdom which is contrary to the wisdom of the Gospels and the spiritual masters.

If we decide to use a sacred text as part of our prayer time, we must realize that reflective spiritual reading differs greatly from the reading of a textbook, a novel, or a newspaper. In fact, if we approach spiritual reading the way we approach the reading of a textbook or novel, we run the risk of creating unnecessary obstacles to God's revelation and touch.

DIFFERENCE BETWEEN INFORMATIVE
AND FORMATIVE READING

Spiritual reading is called *formative,* and the other types of reading are called *informative.* Informative reading makes use of our intellect, or what is sometimes called our "computer intelligence." We read by gathering information or data, analyzing it, comparing it, and categorizing it into neat sections. We usually use the informative approach to scan the newspaper, prepare facts for a meeting, cram for an exam, or master some material we have to teach. This approach is basically utilitarian in nature. Our aim is to gather and manage information that may be useful to us in our daily life. During this process we are in charge. We keep studying a certain text or book until we master it. This type of reading nourishes and satisfies the hunger of the mind to know and to understand things. Most of us have been trained to read or study in this way. Needless to say, the informative approach to reading and to life serves many useful purposes. It enables us to achieve much and bring some kind of order into the chaos of our lives.

In contrast to the informative approach to reading, the reflective, or formative, approach demands a different mindset and a whole new set of attitudes. With this approach, we move into the slow lane of life. There is no reason to feel that we have to get through a certain amount of chapters or pages in one session. On the contrary, we may spend thirty minutes on a few lines of a text. The phrases that are most frequently used to describe the formative approach are: *gentle dwelling, patient abiding, respectful listening, humble openness*, and *receptivity*. We read and gently dwell on the words and phrases of a text. Then we wait with humble openness and receptivity for the Holy Spirit to reveal its hidden treasures. For example, in reflecting on Psalm 23, listen to the Lord say: "I am *your* Shepherd . . . *you* shall not want . . ." and so on.

As mature reflective or formative readers, we are well aware that it is not our cleverness but the power of the Holy Spirit that enables us to receive spiritual food and direction from a given text. We are not in control. Instead we are humble disciples waiting in humble openness for the Master to break open the treasures of a particular text. When we engage in this type of reading, we should always pray to the Holy Spirit for sensitive, spiritual ears to hear the words of the Master. The principle aim is not to analyze, dissect, or gather information out of a sacred passage. The goal of reflective reading is to facilitate spiritual transformation and to allow the sacred words to penetrate our deepest selves for the purpose of spiritual nourishment, illumination, and direction for our lives. Our purpose is to make connections between the text we read and our present life in all its diversity.

We can quickly see that there is quite a difference between the informative and formative approaches to reading. We can also see that if most of the reading we do is of the informative nature, it will not be easy for us to change gears and move into the slow lane of formative reading. We need to remember that spiritual reading is an art to be learned. It involves, among other things, learning to be sensitive to the stirrings of the Spirit as we read, having the discipline to respond to those stirrings, and saying no to the compulsion of our informative side to read quickly and cover as much territory as possible.

SEVEN STAGES OF FORMATIVE READING

Our primary sources of spiritual or sacred reading are Holy Scripture, the spiritual classics, and good contemporary spiritual books. Any of these texts can be a meeting place for us and the Lord where God can speak, illumine, and nourish our deepest selves.

Now that we have examined the characteristics of formative reading, it is imperative that we learn how to read in this way. There are seven stages in the process:

Stage One: Moving in the slow lane and entering the presence of God. Ideally, we should engage in formative reading when our minds are fresh and rested. If we come to sacred reading in a state of overstimulation—with ideas, plans, concerns, anxieties—our minds and hearts will find it difficult, if not impossible, to be receptive. There is so much happening inside us that the "Word" cannot "happen." If we do find ourselves a little tense as we are about to begin a time of formative reading, we can usually help ourselves to relax by taking a few deep breaths and by becoming aware of the presence of God within us. As we begin to relax, we should also try to become aware of and present to all that is going on within us—thoughts, feelings, agitations, whatever. If we are experiencing some tough feelings like anger, apprehension, loneliness, or hurt, we should bring these feelings before Jesus, remembering that he had similar feelings. "In the days when he [Jesus] was in the flesh, he offered prayers and supplications with loud cries and tears to the one who was able to save him from death" (Hebrews 5:7).

Stage Two: Seeking the help of the Holy Spirit. Before he returned to his Father, Jesus said, "The Advocate, the holy Spirit that the Father will send in my name—he will teach you everything and remind you of all that [I] told you" (John 14:26). In his Last Supper discourse, Jesus also said, "Without me you can do nothing" (John 15:5). So, before we begin to reflect on a sacred text (especially a Scripture passage), we need to take a moment to ask the Holy Spirit to guide and inspire our reading, to reveal to us the hidden treasures of this text, and to be open to whatever challenge the sacred words may issue to us. Sometimes our main problem in reading the Scriptures is not that we lack a good method. Our problem is that we do not have the love, the courage, and the generosity to allow God's Word to take possession of our hearts and change our lives.

The next four stages of this process employ the image of a ladder focusing on the four rungs by which we are lifted up to heaven. This "ladder" image is based on the story in Genesis 28:10–22 where Jacob sees a ladder reaching to the heavens. The names of the four rungs of this ladder are:

> *Lectio:* Reading of the Word
> *Meditatio:* Meditation on the Word
> *Oratio:* Praying or responding to the Word that we
> have read and upon which we have meditated
> *Contemplatio:* Contemplating or resting in
> wordless communion with the Word

Stage Three: Lectio—Slowly and prayerfully allowing the Word to enter us. During the *lectio* (reading) stage of our spiritual reading exercise, our aim is simply to be attentive to the words of the chosen text. We are not yet reflecting on them. Our aim is to just allow the words to enter our being—to allow them to soak into our hearts as a gentle rain soaks into the earth. We can continue to read (and reread) slowly the words of the text until some word or phrase grabs hold of us. When this happens we should pause and proceed to the next rung of the ladder—namely, *meditatio*.

Stage Four: Meditatio—Gently dwelling on and reacting to the Word. As we read a text and the Word speaks to us as never before, we are experiencing the gift of the Holy Spirit breaking open for us the meaning of the Word. When this happens we should pause and become present to this "word of salvation," as it is sometimes called. Then we can react to the phrase, sentence, or verse that gripped us. If *lectio* is reading or receiving the Word, *meditatio* is reacting to the Word. Suppose our chosen text was the well-known Emmaus story (see Luke 24:13–35) and the verse that struck us was, "Their eyes were prevented from recognizing him." Our meditation, or reflection, on those words might be: "The two disciples were so absorbed in their own problems that they were unable to recognize the one who joined them. But Jesus was patient. He didn't push the disciples to recognize him. He just walked with them, sensitive to their anguish, waiting patiently for their eyes to be opened." Then we can start to ponder how often in life's journey our eyes are restrained from recognizing Jesus in our midst through an encounter or event in the course of the day. We can become aware of some attitudes in our life, like preoccupation with self, that block us from seeing Jesus.

Our reaction to a different text may be one of confusion;

like the disciples, we might wonder, "What can these words mean?"—anger ("How could Jesus say such a thing?"), joy and consolation, or resistance (when the text challenges our lifestyle and values). When we are finished reacting or reflecting on a text, we are now ready to move to the next rung of the ladder—namely, *oratio*.

Stage Five: Oratio—Responding to the Word spoken to us. Oratio is our response to the Word that the Lord has spoken to us. A passage, verse, or sentence from Scripture or some other spiritual book may have consoled us, inspired us, challenged us, convicted us, or called us to repentance. Now is the time to respond to the Lord about the Word he has given us and upon which we have meditated. The important point here is to be honest when we answer. Our response to the verse in the Emmaus story (see Luke 24:16) might be: "Lord, I become so preoccupied with myself and my concerns that I am often blind to your presence as I walk the journey of life. Please open my eyes to your presence in the people and events of today. Thank you, Lord, for being willing to walk with me in the Emmaus journeys of my life."

Our response to a different text might be: "Lord, I am scared of what you ask of me in this text. I am not ready to give up everything and follow you," and so forth. In times of spiritual dryness, our response might be: "Lord, this Word says nothing to me. I feel so empty. Lord, I find it hard to cope with such emptiness and dryness. I'm afraid that I am losing you. I wonder why you do not come to me. Lord, have mercy and help me to be patient." Such a response will please God very much because it is honest and from the heart.

Stage Six: Contemplatio—Resting with the Word. Contemplatio (contemplation) is regarded as the highest form of prayer. It is present when we stop reading (*lectio*), thinking (*meditatio*), and speaking (*oratio*), and begin resting silently in the Lord's presence. It is like the experience of two friends enjoying each other's presence without speaking. They may turn to each other in an embrace of wordless communication. In contemplation we are aware that we are in God and he is in us, and that is all we need right now. After our period of *contemplatio*, if time permits, we may begin the process all over again. We begin to read again (Stage Three) until some word strikes us. Then we pause and reflect on it, repeating the entire process.

Stage Seven: Concluding with a prayer of thanksgiving. We should end our formative reading time with a prayer of thanksgiving. We can give thanks to the Lord for any insights received or for the experience of his loving presence. We should give thanks even if we think we received nothing and are being sent away empty. We may well have received many spiritual gifts, especially the great gift of learning to love and remain faithful to prayer in spite of a lack of any tangible sign of God's presence and activity.

There are two points to keep in mind when we use this type of prayer. First, if we keep a spiritual journal, we may want to keep a log of the texts, the "words of salvation," that we receive from the Lord in formative reading. These "words of salvation" can be read over and over and allowed to nour-ish, illumine, and give direction to our deepest self.

Second, if while reflecting on a certain text—for exam-ple, the one about turning the other cheek—we find ourselves struggling with the message, we should stay with it and try to become aware of the reasons we are resisting it. "Is the text asking too much of me?" "Is it questioning some attitude or behavior that I don't want to let go of?" "Do I simply have a hard time believing the truth of the text?"

We should also talk to the Lord about the text, telling him of our problems with it. We may initially feel ashamed or em-barrassed at our resistance and find it difficult to talk openly to the Lord. At such times we should remember that Jesus, who struggled in Gethsemane with what his Father was asking of him, will most surely understand our struggles and resistance. This is where honesty in prayer is vital. There is always the temptation to avoid talking about hard and unpleasant mat-ters in our lives. But if our relationship with God (and other people) is going to be real, we must do all that we can to lay all our cards on the table.

The format described here is only one way to do formative reading; there are many other variations. Readers are urged to use the parts of this format that help them to make the sacred text a meeting place for the reader and the Lord. Whatever facilitates that meeting is a good method. Whatever hinders that meeting is a bad method.

Questions for Personal Reflection and Small-Group Discussion

1. What spoke to you most in this chapter?
2. How do you read a spiritual text? Could your way of reading be enriched in any way by the seven-step method offered in this chapter?
3. When reading or listening to the Word of God in the Bible, do you ever experience "resistance" to certain texts? If so, how do you usually handle the situation?
4. What was your experience with the suggested prayer exercise offered below?

Suggested Prayer Exercise

Take a passage of Scripture or a passage from a spiritual book and reflect on it, using the format described in this chapter. When you are finished, spend a few minutes identifying what you liked and did not like about the format.

TEN

Prayer of Contemplation

*All of us, gazing with unveiled face on the glory of the
Lord, are being transformed into the same image from
glory to glory, as from the Lord who is the Spirit.*

2 CORINTHIANS 3:18

*The first task in life is prayer, not the prayer
of words, like a parrot, but the prayer of
the heart; gazing on the Lord. . . .*

POPE FRANCIS

The majority of Christians do not think that contemplative prayer is for "ordinary Christians." Most people would
tend to say, "That's only for monks and religious who live
in monasteries." Perhaps the reason why many of us think
that way is because we have preconceived concepts of contemplative prayer as something very lofty, mystical, and far
beyond the capacity of the ordinary Christian. On the contrary, contemplative prayer is possible for anyone who is interested in becoming *more aware* of the realities encountered
in everyday life. It is possible for anyone who is willing to
stop being *constantly on the go* to *being still* in contemplative

prayer before the God who is the Ground of all being. Furthermore, contemplative prayer is something that most of us have experienced or done without actually calling it by that name.

In his book *Seeking the Face of God,* William Shannon describes contemplation this way: "Contemplation is being in the presence of God and letting go of thoughts, images, desires, concerns, anxieties. I let go of all that is not God so that I can truly experience the presence of God. . . . [Contemplation] is simply achieving a deep awareness of what always has been and is true of me: namely, that I am in God, as everything that is, is in God."

The image of sunbathing can also help us to understand what contemplative prayer is and how we can go about doing it. When we sunbathe, we lie under the sun and allow its warmth to penetrate our bodies. In sunbathing our only task is to "let it happen"—to make ourselves available and vulnerable to the sun and enjoy its warm touch upon our bodies. So it is with contemplative prayer. Our task is to be open and receptive to the warm touch of God's love. We need do nothing but be receptive to what God offers us. A popular story in prayer circles tells of an old farmer who used to spend a lot of time in church sitting quietly in the presence of the Blessed Sacrament. One day his pastor asked him how he spent his time—what he did while in prayer. The old farmer simply answered, "I look at him and he looks at me." His prayer was one of being available to and enjoying the presence of God.

Every person is born with a potential to contemplate;

but, like much else in life, that potential must be nourished and fostered or it will lie dormant. We will now look at three prayers that can help to foster and nourish the contemplative dimension of our being.

PRAYER OF APPRECIATION
FOR GOD'S CREATION

The most natural and perhaps the easiest way for us to develop our contemplative side is by taking time to grow in our awareness and appreciation of God's creation. Our Divine Artist has given us much to admire. An excellent way to thank God for his handiwork is by admiring and appreciating what he has created. When we attend an art festival and take the time to admire a piece of art, we can be sure that our admiration gives the artist pleasure even if we never verbally express our pleasure. The very fact that we take time to look at, touch, and show appreciation for artists' creations establishes a communication between them and us.

So it is when we take time to admire and appreciate God's creation. God is pleased when we stop to gaze at the beauty of a sunrise or sunset, smell a flower, or watch a child at play. The Irish poet Padraic Pearse gives us an example of contemplative appreciation of creation when he writes:

Sometimes my heart hath shaken with
Great joy

To see a leaping squirrel in a tree.
Or a lady-bird upon a stalk,
Or little rabbits in a field at evening,
Lit by a slanting sun. . . .
Or children with bare feet upon
The sands
Of some ebbed sea, or playing on the
Streets
Of little towns in Connacht. . . .

Another beautiful description of the human person contemplating the wonder of God's creation is found in Psalm 8. Perhaps one evening the psalmist was out for a stroll, and as he contemplated the star-filled sky, he was filled with awe and wonder. He expressed what was within him in this way:

O Lord, our Lord, . . .
When I behold your heavens, the work of your fingers,
the moon and the stars which you set in place —
What is man that you should be mindful of him, or the
son of man that you should care for him?
You have made him little less than the angels, and
crowned him with glory and honor. . . .
O Lord, our Lord,
how glorious is your name over all
the earth! (Psalm 8:2,4–6,10)

Poets and artists have a special talent for expressing their admiration for creation, but God must be equally pleased by our more mundane expressions of delight. By taking time to smell the flowers, behold a sunrise or sunset, or admire a tree, a seashell, or a painting, we are developing in a very natural way our capacity for contemplative prayer.

CENTERING PRAYER

Centering prayer is quite popular among Protestant and Catholic Christians alike. One of its greatest modern proponents was a Cistercian monk, Fr. Basil Pennington. He described it in his book entitled *Centering Prayer: Renewing an Ancient Christian Prayer Form*:

> In Centering Prayer we go beyond thought and image, beyond the senses of the rational mind, to that center of our being where God is working a wonderful work. There God our Father is not only bringing us forth at each moment in his wonderful creative love, but by virtue of the grace of filiation, which we received at Baptism, he is indeed making us sons and daughters, one with his own Son, pouring out in our hearts the Spirit of his Son, so that we can in the fullest sense cry, "Abba Father." He says to us in fact more than in word, "You are my son; this day I have begotten you." At this level of our being where we are our truest selves, we are essen-

tially prayer, total response to the Father in our oneness with the Son, in that love who is the Holy Spirit.

We can read this statement and say, "How beautiful!" But the important point is to *experience* what it says—that is, to actually see ourselves as beloved sons and daughters of the Father and really feel the indwelling of the Father, Son, and Holy Spirit at our deepest center. Centering Prayer is one of the best means we can use to facilitate the attainment of such an experience. By frequently taking time to find our center point, we gradually, through the grace of God, come to know experientially the Lord who lives in the center of our being, the One who is our deepest center. In centering prayer we become present to the God within and we love him from our deepest center.

How can we learn to pray in this way? Both Basil Pennington and Thomas Keating have written extensively about Centering Prayer and how to practice it. The four steps or stages which follow are drawn mainly from their writings.

Stage One: Find a quiet place and take a few minutes to relax. This can be done by slowly inhaling and exhaling. Sitting in a straight-backed chair is the recommended posture for this form of prayer.

Stage Two: Once we feel relaxed, we can make an act of faith to become aware of the presence of God within us. We may wish to pray the following or a similar act of faith:

Lord Jesus, I believe that you are truly present at the center of my being, bringing me forth in your love.

During this prayer period I want to be completely present to you. Draw me into your loving presence and help me to experience myself as your beloved child.

Stage Three: We need to center our whole attention on God, allowing him alone to be the sole concern of our mind and heart. The anonymous author of the fourteenth-century spiritual classic, *The Cloud of Unknowing*, proposes this method:

> This is what you are to do: Lift your heart to the Lord with a gentle stirring of love, desiring him for his own sake and not for his gifts. Center all your attention and desire on him and let this be the sole concern of your mind and heart. Do all in your power to forget everything else, keeping your thoughts and desires free from involvement with any of God's creatures or their affairs whether in general or in particular.

The anonymous author of *The Cloud of Unknowing* is regarded as the originator or creator of the prayer form we call centering prayer.

If our mind begins to wander, as it most surely will, it is helpful to choose and use a single word (sometimes called a prayer word or mantra) to help us ward off the distractions and keep our minds and hearts on God alone. Many people who practice Centering Prayer choose a prayer word such as peace, love, truth, or Abba. When we are distracted by other images, thoughts, or insights, however noble or spiritual, we should begin to use our prayer word as a means of keeping our entire attention on God. Once focused on God we can allow our prayer word to recede into the background. In other words, we need only use the prayer word to ward off distractions until we once again turn our focus back to God. Some days we may be so plagued with distractions that we will have to use the prayer word constantly to bring us back on track.

When we sit at the feet of the Lord, he may seem more absent than present. Other days we may be able to stay at the center with little or no effort. It is important that we do not judge a prayer period that is free of distractions as being better and more pleasing to God than a prayer period that has no distractions. A distractionless prayer period is obviously more satisfying but not necessarily more pleasing to God. What God looks for in prayer is a heart that longs for him, seeks him, and cries out for union with him. If we have that thought in prayer, then our prayer, regardless of the number of distractions, is very pleasing to God. Also, when dealing with distractions, we should remember that every decision to turn away from a distraction in order to turn back to God is a decision to love. If during a particular prayer time we turn away fifty times from distractions in order to turn back to God, we can say we have made fifty acts of love. Surely this would be most pleasing to God.

Stage Four: It is suggested that the Centering Prayer period end with a slow recitation of the Lord's Prayer. We may also want to ask the Lord to help us to continue moving through the rest of our day with a sense of God's loving presence.

If we tend to be achievers and doers, we may find Centering Prayer difficult. We may think it is a waste of time and wonder what is the point of just sitting there doing nothing. Centering Prayer is a symbolic way of saying that spiritual growth is the work of God and not of the one who prays. We become holy not so much by our doing but by allowing God to transform us.

THE JESUS PRAYER

The Jesus Prayer is another ancient prayer form that has been rediscovered in recent times. Even though the prayer involves using some words, it can still be considered as a contemplative prayer form. (Contemplative prayer is usually described as a *wordless* form of prayer.) The traditional wording of the Jesus Prayer is this: "Lord Jesus, have mercy on me, a sinner." It is based on Luke 18:14 and 18:39. Some people shorten it to "Jesus, have mercy on me," or simply "Jesus." The prayer has been used by Christians—especially Eastern Christian monks—since at least the fourth century. The desert fathers used it to implement Christ's exhortation to pray without ceasing. Mahatma Gandhi, who was a zealous advocate of this form of prayer, claimed that it brought with it the most extraordinary benefits for spirit, mind, and body. He claimed to have overcome all his fears, even as a child, simply through the ceaseless repetition of God's name. Gandhi has said that there was more power in its recitation than in the atom bomb.

The Jesus Prayer has always been linked with breathing because breath symbolizes the Spirit or life of God within us. As we inhale and say, "Lord Jesus," we can imagine ourselves taking in the love and presence of Jesus and all that is good and beautiful. As we exhale and say, "Have mercy on me, a sinner," we can imagine ourselves breathing out of our systems everything that is destructive to our well-being and growth.

While this is one valid way to pray the Jesus Prayer, we should remember that we don't have to synchronize it with our breathing. Some people like to synchronize the prayer with their breathing, but others find this concentration a distraction. Either way is good. We need only find a formula and rhythm that is good for us.

We can use the Jesus Prayer in both spousal and occupational situations. In spousal prayer we will begin our formal time with the Lord by spending a few minutes saying the Jesus Prayer. We take a few moments to "center down" (to become present to Jesus who dwells with us), and then we begin to rhythmically pray or chant the Jesus Prayer. Many people report that this prayer has a tremendously calming and healing effect on their lives.

In occupational prayer we can also use the Jesus Prayer as we go about the duties of our day. As we drive to work in the morning, we can repeat slowly, "Jesus, have mercy on me," or "Jesus, have mercy on all the people I meet this day." As we go about our work at home or wait in line at the store or at the doctor's office, we can pray the Jesus Prayer. When we participate in meetings that are beginning to produce more heat than light, we can pray the Jesus Prayer. We can pray it when we wake up in the middle of the night. Veteran users of the prayer tell how they actually wake up with this prayer on their lips. It has become one with their breathing. From all this, we can see how regular use of the Jesus Prayer will foster in us a spirit of contemplation.

CONTEMPLATIVE MOMENTS

To conclude this chapter on contemplative prayer, something should be said about what can be called the "gift of a contemplative moment," which is another name for a religious experience. A contemplative moment is the experience of suddenly and spontaneously finding ourselves caught up in the presence of God. Suddenly, unexpectedly, and without perhaps consciously asking for it, we find ourselves loved, embraced, and cherished by God. We have a deep feeling of inner peace and a sense of connectedness with all of creation. Such graced moments may happen as we walk down the street, take a stroll on the beach, sit at our desk, hold a small baby in our arms, sit alone in church, paint a picture, dance, look into a microscope, or whatever. Fr. William Barry gives us two examples of contemplative moments in his book, *God and You*. He writes:

> A man was walking along a beach at night and saw the moonlight touch with silver the crest of a wave.

He was delighted and felt at peace and in the presence of someone who himself delights in such things. He felt that God was close and loved him even though he often drank too much and got angry with his family. He knew that God knew all about him and yet loved him, and he felt freer than he had in years.

Recently I was walking near the seashore. It was a bright, crisp autumn day; the sun shone through golden and red leaves and sparkled on the blue water. All of a sudden I felt a tremendous sense of well-being, a great gratitude and a strong desire welling up in me. On reflection I knew that I had felt the touch of God and a strong desire for him.

While such graced moments of contemplation are indeed the free gift of God, we can facilitate their coming by engaging in any of the three examples of prayer outlined in this chapter. These three models of contemplative prayer do indeed facilitate the gift of experiencing communion with God, but we should not be overly concerned with following a particular method. Rather, we should concern ourselves with having a heart that seeks union with its Maker. We should concentrate on creating space in our lives to ponder and be present to the loving presence of God. The extent and quality of our presence to God, the Ground of being, will greatly determine the quality of our presence to people.

Questions for Personal Reflection and Small-Group Discussion

1. What spoke to you most in this chapter?
2. Have you ever spent time contemplating the beauty of creation? If so, how was that experience for you?
3. Have you ever done centering prayer or the Jesus Prayer? If so, how was that experience for you?
4. Have you ever experienced contemplative moments similar to the ones described in this chapter?
5. What was your experience with the suggested prayer exercise offered below?

Suggested Prayer Exercise

Do one of the forms of contemplation offered in this chapter.

ELEVEN

Prayer of Adoration

Jesus said to Peter, "Simon, are you asleep?
Could you not keep watch for one hour? Watch
and pray that you may not undergo the test.
The spirit is willing but the flesh is weak."

MARK 14:34–38

Adoration means entering the depth of our hearts
in communion with the Lord, who makes Himself
bodily present in the Eucharist. In the monstrance,
he always entrusts Himself to us and asks us to be
united with his presence, with his Risen Body.

POPE BENEDICT XVI

Prayer before Jesus in the Blessed Sacrament, outside of Mass, occurs in the Catholic Church in several ways—e.g., during the benediction service; before the Eucharistic presence of Jesus in a closed tabernacle in the church; or before a monstrance that holds the Eucharist in the Adoration Chapel.

Simply put, Eucharistic adoration is prayer in the presence of Jesus in the Eucharist. While we can and should spend time with Jesus in our homes and elsewhere, his presence in the Eucharist is, in a sense, more real than elsewhere. It's a bit like the difference between speaking to someone on the phone or behind a screen and speaking to someone face-to-face.

We call Eucharistic adoration "perpetual" when adoration goes on 24/7 in a chapel located on parish grounds. Parishioners who sign up commit to praying for one hour—or more—each week in the chapel. Since July 2002, when our chapel was blessed and opened, we have had prayer on our parish and school campus twenty-four hours a day, seven days a week.

During our recent annual renewal sign-up for perpetual adoration, two of our adorers witnessed to the importance of this form of prayer in their lives. Clara Centeno-Calero, wife and mother of young children and a manager at her place of work, said:

> Going to the Adoration Chapel has helped me grow spiritually in a way I cannot describe with words. It is truly a special place where Jesus is waiting for us to come and spend time with him. He is always waiting, and he is waiting for *you*.

John Casko, a retired man, expressed his joy for signing up a year ago to spend an hour weekly before Jesus in the Blessed Sacrament. He wrote:

> I am so amazed at the positive effect that the past year of adoration is having for me! So many times I've cho-

sen a book at random and found something in it that directly related to events in our family life. I walk out of the chapel knowing that God is with me and will help me face whatever comes my way. I started out wondering how to fit the hour into my schedule; now I happily schedule everything else around adoration. Life gets easy when you get your priorities straight.

Even if your parish does not have a perpetual adoration chapel, you could consider spending an hour a week or even a half hour each week in prayer before Jesus in the Blessed Sacrament in your church. The following are six reasons to consider spending an hour each week with Jesus in the Blessed Sacrament.

1. It is an *act of generosity* which makes us a little more like our generous God. Too many of us are stingy with our time when it comes to the most important relationship in life.
2. It is not only good for us spiritually; it is also good for our mental, emotional, and physical well-being.
3. It gives us a great opportunity to spend quality time reading God's Word or some other good spiritual book.
4. It is a way to just *hang out* with the One who *knows us best and loves us most*—the One who paid the ultimate price for our salvation.

5. It is a wonderful way to spend time thinking and praying about our lives, relationships, and anxieties. It also gives us the opportunity to pray for our family, our country, and many global issues.

6. It is a wonderful preparation for heaven. If we are reluctant to *waste time* with Jesus here on earth, what do we think it will be like to spend eternity with him?

SUGGESTIONS FOR SPENDING QUIET TIME WITH JESUS

When people are asked to consider spending thirty minutes or an hour with Jesus, they often ask: "What would I do? How do I spend that time?" As you will see, the following suggestions can help, whether we are praying in the adoration chapel, in the church before a closed tabernacle, or in our homes.

Suggestion #1: Take a moment to consciously become aware of God's presence. In the adoration chapel or in church, people usually begin their time of prayer by kneeling down before Jesus. For me personally, after taking a moment to consciously become aware of Jesus' presence, I address the Father, Son, and Holy Spirit. I thank the Father for the many years of good life he has given me, for all the spiritual and material blessings of my life, and for my priesthood. I thank Jesus for paying the ultimate price for our salvation and for being our good and caring Shepherd. I thank the Holy Spirit for the countless number of ways he has guided me and helped me in my journey. Most importantly, I ask Jesus for the help I need to pray well during this holy hour.

Suggestion #2. Become aware of the thoughts and feelings we are bringing to this time of prayer. Our thoughts and feelings are a part of the true self we are bringing to this time of prayer. We should take a moment to become aware of what is going on within us at this time. Are we happy, trustful, sad, or fearful? We bring to prayer whatever mood we are in.

Suggestion #3. Spend some quiet time sitting in the loving presence of Jesus. This is an aspect of prayer that many of us may be uncomfortable with simply because we find it difficult to just sit quietly and do nothing. The doing or active part of us may drive us to think that sitting quietly and doing nothing is a waste of valuable time. If we have a hard time *doing nothing* in prayer, we may need to remember the lovely words of Psalm 46:10, "Be still and know that I am God." A medieval mystic once said: "While we rest in him, he works in us." If we tend to be a busybody during our time of prayer, the above words should help us to see the value of resting in the Lord.

Many will say: "When I try to be *still*, my mind wanders." I understand. I face this challenge every time I try to be still. Here are a couple of important things to keep in mind regarding distractions. We need to distinguish between *silly* or unimportant *distractions* (e.g., outside noises, who will win the football game this week, etc.) and distractions that are very much connected with our lives (e.g., a difficult relationship, anxiety over health, or a financial situation). Sometimes we are called to *pray* about a particular distraction, to take it to

God and seek his help and guidance. But sometimes we may feel that we want to put a particular issue aside so we can focus our attention on the Lord. On the issue of distractions, St. Francis de Sales said:

> If the heart wanders or is distracted, bring it back quite gently and place it tenderly in God's presence. And if you do nothing else while at prayer but bring your heart back again and again and place it in God's presence, . . . though it went away every time you brought it back, your time of prayer would be very well spent.

The devil will *not* want us to believe these encouraging words. But we do need to believe them. Sometimes in prayer, we may feel that we are being *sent away empty.* But if we have made a decent attempt to remain focused on Jesus, we should believe that he is indeed pleased with us. If our only focus is on what we are *getting out* of our prayer time (a consumerist mentality), we will end up feeling that this is *a waste of our valuable time.* On the other hand, if we can come to the chapel *not* primarily to *receive* but to *give* Jesus some of our time and attention, we may discover the truth of the words: "In giving we receive." Just wanting to *hang out with Jesus*, to *waste time with him,* is a blessed and wonderful attitude to have.

Suggestion #4. Engage in spiritual reading. As stated in an earlier chapter, spiritual reading (often called *lectio divina*) nourishes, illumines, and gives direction to our deepest self. If we have time to read the newspaper, emails, and Facebook, surely we can make time for spiritual reading.

Spiritual reading should always be slow and meditative. When something strikes us, we should pause and sit with the word that is speaking to our soul. As we grow spiritually, we will find that a few verses of Scripture or a paragraph in a good book will be all we need during a quiet time with the Lord.

Suggestion #5. Conclude with prayers of petition, intercession, and thanksgiving. Most likely, all of us who spend time in prayer bring up our own intentions (prayers of petition) and the intentions of others (intercessory prayers). Finally, it is always good to end our time with the Lord with a prayer of thanksgiving: "Thank you, Jesus, for this time of prayer. Help me to keep a sense of your presence through the rest of this day."

Persevering in prayer. Perseverance is a virtue we all need when it comes to most things, including dieting, exercising, or staying in a difficult relationship. Persevering in prayer is also a challenge, especially when we think it is a waste of time, or when we feel God is not answering our prayer. We can be certain that the devil's agenda is always to get us to quit whatever it is that will help us to become better. It is easy enough to be persuaded that we could use our time better than sitting with the Lord. What we need is to be strongly convinced of the value of *wasting time with the Lord.*

Questions for Personal Reflection and Small-Group Discussion

1. What spoke to you most in this chapter?
2. Is Eucharistic adoration a dimension of your spiritual life? If so, what drew you to it? If not, what keeps you from trying this form of prayer?
3. Is setting aside a quiet time to be alone with the Lord a part of your spiritual life? If so, what motivated you to commit to such quiet time? If not, what blocks you from committing yourself to frequent quiet times with the Lord?
4. What was your experience with the suggested prayer exercise offered below?

Suggested Spiritual Exercise

If possible, spend an hour in prayer in the presence of Jesus in the adoration chapel. If there is no adoration chapel in your area, spend thirty minutes or an hour in quiet time in your church or home. Follow the format suggested above and see how it works for you.

TWELVE

Praying the Rosary

"Hail, favored one! The Lord is with you.
. . . Most blessed are you among women,
and blessed is the fruit of your womb."

LUKE 1:28,42

The Rosary has accompanied me in moments of joy
and in moments of difficulty. To it I have entrusted
any number of concerns; in it I have always found
comfort. The Rosary is my favorite prayer. It is
marvelous in its simplicity and in its depths.

ST. JOHN PAUL II

When I was growing up in the countryside of Ireland (a place dotted with shrines to our Blessed Mother), the family Rosary was a must. There was never a valid reason for missing it. If someone was sick in bed, we gathered in that person's room to pray the beads. The family Rosary was often said as we all traveled in a car to or from the homes of friends or relatives. My experience was not uncommon. A unique mark of Catholicism was its loyalty to the Rosary as a way of honoring Mary and reflecting on the joyful, sorrowful, and glorious events in her Son's life.

The widespread popularity of the Rosary fell off after Vatican II—an unintended consequence of the Council's efforts to refocus Catholics on Jesus, the Scripture, and the liturgy. But as Pope John Paul rightly noted in his Apostolic Letter *Rosarium Virginis Mariae*, while the Rosary is "clearly Marian in character, at heart it is a Christocentric prayer" and "has all the depth of the Gospel message in its entirety."

ORIGIN OF THE ROSARY

No one knows for certain how the Rosary began. A pious tradition held that Mary appeared to St. Dominic and gave him the Rosary. While this tradition is seriously questioned today, we do know that the Dominicans were very involved in the standardizing and popularizing of this prayer. Pope Pius V, a Dominican, instituted the Feast of Our Lady of the Rosary (currently celebrated on October 7). He also credited the efficacy of the Rosary with the defeat of the Turks at the Battle of Lepanto in 1571.

But before all this, around the year 1,000 A.D., ordinary laypeople developed the practice of praying 150 Our Fathers divided into three sets of fifty. In doing this, they were copying the monks who prayed the 150 psalms. They counted the Our Fathers with the help of beads. This form of prayer became known as the "poor man's psalter." As Marian devotion spread in the twelfth century, the Hail Mary prayer was added. The first part of the Hail Mary is based on the Angel Gabriel's greeting to Mary (Luke 1:28, 43). Thereafter, the Church added the second part: "Holy Mary, Mother of God, pray for us sinners now and at the hour of our death. Amen." Each decade of the Rosary was prayed with one Our Father, ten Hail Marys, and one Glory Be to the Father.

In praying the Rosary, Catholics are neither worshipping Mary nor ignoring Jesus. Rather, we are asking Mary to intercede for us, just as we ask other Christians to pray for us.

TWENTY MYSTERIES

In time, the tradition developed into a reflection of the various events in the life of Jesus as one prayed the decades of the Rosary. Until quite recently, we reflected on three sets of five mysteries: the Joyful, Sorrowful, and Glorious Mysteries. The Joyful Mysteries focus on the birth of Christ, the Sorrowful Mysteries on his passion and death, and the Glorious Mysteries on his resurrection and ascension into heaven.

In 2002, Pope John Paul added a new set of five mysteries called the Luminous Mysteries (or the Mysteries of Light), the focus of which is the public life of Jesus from his birth to his institution of the Eucharist. The Joyous Mysteries are prayed on Monday and Saturday, the Sorrowful Mysteries on Tuesday and Friday, the Luminous Mysteries on Thursday, and the Glorious Mysteries on Wednesday and Sunday.

In his 2002 Apostolic Letter on the Rosary, St. John Paul said that Mary lived with her eyes fixed on Christ, treasuring his every word. When praying the Rosary, we join with Mary in contemplating key events in the life of Jesus and in our salvation. John Paul says: "Without this contemplative dimension, the Rosary loses its meaning. Without contemplation, the Rosary is a body without a soul, and its recitation runs the risk of becoming a mechanical repletion of formulas." So as we make our way through the various mysteries of the Rosary, Mary is our companion and guide, leading us to appreciate ever more deeply such events as the Annunciation, the Wedding Feast at Cana, Jesus' Death on the Cross, the Descent of the Holy Spirit on the Apostles, and so on.

THE ROSARY: A WAY TO PRAY FOR PERSONAL, LOCAL, AND GLOBAL INTENTIONS

I have come to see the mysteries of the Rosary as not only a great way to focus our attention on important events in the lives of Jesus and Mary, but also to pray for personal, local, and global intentions. The following are some examples from all four sets of mysteries.

The Annunciation (Luke 1:26–38)—First Joyful Mystery. As we contemplate the Angel Gabriel's visit to Mary, we can pray for the grace to say "yes" to God's call; for couples seeking to conceive or adopt a child; for all women who have recently miscarried or aborted a child; for women experiencing a painful and difficult pregnancy; that those considering abortion will chose life; for the conversion of pro-choice advocates.

Finding of Jesus in the Temple (Luke 2:41–50)—Fifth Joyful Mystery. As we contemplate both the anxiety and joy of Mary and Joseph in this event, we can pray for missing children and their families; for children and teenagers forced into slave labor and prostitution; for the conversion of those who harm children.

Scourging at the Pillar (Matthew 27:26)—Second Sorrowful Mystery. As we contemplate this horrible event, we can pray for the victims of domestic and street violence; for victims of war, torture, and terrorism; for the conversion of terrorists and extremists; for the safety of all engaged in the war against terrorism; for an end to war.

Jesus Carries His Cross (Mark 15:21–22)—Fourth Sorrowful Mystery. While meditating on this event, we can pray for those carrying a big cross at this time and for their loved ones and caregivers; that the crosses of life will make us better, not bitter; for all who have asked us to pray for them; for those who will receive bad news today.

Wedding Feast of Cana (John 2:1–12)—Second Luminous Mystery. As we meditate on this happy event, we can pray for engaged and married couples; for hurting couples, that they will reach out for divine and human help; for all involved in marriage and family life ministry.

Transfiguration (Luke 9:28–36)—Fourth Luminous Mystery. As we contemplate on this mystery, we can pray that we, like the apostles, may listen to Jesus and be transfigured into his likeness; for those who work in houses of prayer and formation; for those who are seeking change; for those who are discerning a vocation.

Resurrection (Mark 16:1–20)—First Glorious Mystery. As we meditate on this mystery, we can pray for God's blessing on all those fighting the forces of evil in our world: poverty, terrorism, the culture of death, injustices; for a spiritual awakening of those who are spiritually asleep; for those who will be preaching in churches this weekend.

Crowning of Mary, Queen of Heaven (Revelation 12:1)— Fifth Glorious Mystery. As we contemplate on Mary's coronation, we can pray for leaders of nations; for the conversion of unbelievers; for our own ongoing conversion; for an increase of true devotion to Mary; for all who have asked us to pray for them.

(For a complete list of intentions attached to all twenty mysteries of the Rosary, visit my parish website, www.ascensioncatholic.net; select Fr. Tobin's writings and click on Miscellaneous Articles.)

The late Fr. Joseph Champlin, in *Behind Closed Doors,* writes that he sometimes uses the five decades of the Rosary to pray for the people of the five major continents of the world. As he prays each decade, he thinks of the Church and the people on a particular continent, with their needs, burdens, and joys. This way of praying the Rosary would certainly give our prayer a universal touch. As we move our way through each bead of the rosary, we meet, as it were, and pray for people all over the world.

The Rosary can also be prayed communally during a

family gathering, the gathering of several families, or a parish gathering. In his *America* article (May 1983), Mitch Finley describes how he, his wife, and several couples gathered together to pray God's blessing on their marriages. He writes:

> A few weeks ago, my wife and I joined eight other married couples for prayer. We began a series of gatherings to pray for marriage in general, and for marriages in particular—our own and those of couples we know who seem in need of some prayer right about now. A small purpose, really, but one with vast implications.
>
> We lit the living room with fluttering candles and, yes, prayed the rosary—not without self-consciousness, to be sure, since none of us had thought of ourselves as rosary types for a good long time.
>
> What a remarkable thing, I thought to myself. We gathered, greeted one another, and here we are right away praying. We did not spend several meetings trying to agree on how to pray, first.

When such groups gather to pray the Rosary, each decade could be preceded with a short reading and concluded with a verse of a sacred song.

St. Paul writes: "Have no anxiety at all, but in everything, by prayer and petition, with thanksgiving, make your requests known to God" (Philippians 4:6). The Rosary is certainly one very valid form of prayer that can be used to present our needs to God. If we decide to pray the Rosary in some of these creative ways, we may be following the Lord's exhortation by becoming a disciple "who brings from his storeroom both the new and the old" (Matthew 13:52). Spiritual renewal involves, among other things, taking old things out of our spiritual storeroom and using them in new ways that speak to people living in a new age.

Questions for Personal Reflection and Small-Group Discussion

1. What spoke to you most in this chapter?
2. What has been your experience with the Rosary, past and present?
3. Which, if any, of the above suggestions could enhance your Rosary prayer?
4. What was your experience with the suggested prayer exercise offered below?

Suggested Prayer Exercise

Pray the Rosary using one of the creative ways suggested in this chapter. Also identify an intention for each decade you pray.

THIRTEEN

Prayer in Times of Spiritual Dryness

*The Lord, your God, will circumcise your hearts
... that you may love the Lord, your God, with all
your heart and all your soul, and so may live.*

DEUTERONOMY 30:6

*It may be useless—and perhaps a source of still
greater agitation—to want to seek assurance
that we are in the grace of God and what we are
experiencing [a time of spiritual dryness] is only a
trial, and not abandonment on the part of God. At
such times it is God's will that we should not have
this assurance. And he does this so that we may
humble ourselves more and increase our prayers
and acts of confidence in his mercy. We desire
to see, and God wills that we should not see.*

St. Alphonsus Liguori

Sooner or later in our prayers we experience what is called *dryness*—a time when we have no sense of God's presence. We may even think we have lost our Beloved or feel abandoned by God. In the school of prayer, few things are more important to understand than the nature and role of spiritual dryness.

There are six significant questions that should be asked about prayer during these desert experiences, as they are sometimes called.

Question One: What is it that praying people experience during the desert or dry periods of the spiritual journey?

The actual desert experience will vary depending on the person's level of faith and spiritual maturity. For the beginner in prayer, spiritual dryness frequently means not just the absence of a *felt sense* of the presence of God but also feelings of what St. Ignatius calls desolation—that is, states of anxiousness, sadness, or loss of peace flowing from the thought that "I have lost God" or "God has abandoned me."

On the other hand, for the person who is more mature in faith and advanced in the ways of prayer, spiritual dryness may not be an experience of desolation. It will be one which lacks a felt sense of God's presence but may be accompanied by the conviction: "Even though I can't feel God's presence (at least on the external level), I do believe the Lord is close and active in my life. Even though I cannot feel his presence (the state of spiritual dryness), I don't feel anxious, sad, or abandoned (the state of desolation). In fact, I feel peaceful." (See *Weeds Among the Wheat* and *When the Well Runs Dry* by Thomas H. Green, for more information on this topic.)

To believe that God is present and active despite his apparent absence can be considered one of the greatest blessings of the spiritual life. For most of us, particularly in the early years of prayer, spiritual dryness usually includes the experience of desolation ("I have lost God; God has abandoned me"). Usually it is a time of spiritual suffering. We think we are getting the "silent treatment" from God. We call out to him all day long, but he never answers (see Psalm 22:3). Spiritual dryness is like journeying in the desert with no water in sight. Prayer is no longer exciting; rather, it is a wearying struggle. Spiritual exercises that once nourished us now are empty, and we have little or no desire to do them.

Another dimension of the desert experience may be a feeling of discouragement as we become keenly aware of our own sinfulness. (We may not yet know that one of the surest signs of growth in the interior life is a growing awareness of our own sinfulness.) We may begin to think we are regressing rather than progressing. We may begin to experience one of the great paradoxes of the spiritual life: The closer we come to God, the farther it seems to us that we are away from him. As we get closer to the all-piercing Light of God, the more our own darkness will show itself. Our lives will appear to be hollow and mediocre. The late Fr. John Dalrymple, in his book *Simple Prayer*, writes:

It is as if I were to bring the sleeve of my coat toward the window of the room, and as I move into the light, the dust and dandruff on the sleeve become more obvious. It is not that as I moved the coat got dirtier, but that the light got brighter.

What seems to scare and hurt us most is the thought that we have lost our Beloved and that he has abandoned us (see Song of Songs 3:1–11). This thought or feeling characterizes the experience of desolation described earlier.

To sum up, it can be said that while the actual experience of the desert will be different for different people, for all of us it will mean a felt sense of the absence of God. And for those of us whose faith in God is still fragile, it will frequently involve the experience of desolation (the "I have lost God" feeling).

This description of spiritual dryness may give the impression that it is something experienced only by monks, religious, and exceptional laypersons. Yet spiritual directors maintain that this experience is quite common in the lives of many average, prayerful laypeople who discover somewhere in the midst of their spiritual journeys that spiritual exercises, which once nourished them immensely now do nothing for them.

Question Two: Why is an understanding of this dimension of prayer so important?

There are at least three reasons why some understanding of spiritual dryness is important.

First, if we do not understand the role of the desert in the spiritual life, we may quit praying in times of dryness. We may think that we have "lost God" and that our prior, positive feelings in prayer were not a gift from God but the creation of our own imaginations. This frequently happens. Many people experience genuine conversion and get all excited about prayer, but they quit when the well runs dry. This is sad because it is often at that time that God wants to do his real work in such persons.

Second, lack of knowledge about the purpose of spiritual dryness may cause us to continue praying in a way that, *at this particular stage in our spiritual journey*, may be more of an obstacle than a help to our spiritual growth. Many people are unaware that at some stage in the spiritual journey God may call them to become less active in prayer so he can be more active in their spiritual transformation.

Third, the experience of spiritual dryness may either be caused by ourselves or something permitted by God. When it is permitted by God, it is meant to purify us and bring us closer to him. Such dryness is a gift to be accepted and embraced. When spiritual dryness is our doing, we need to work at removing the causes of such dryness. Lack of knowledge about the nature and role of spiritual dryness may lead us to believe that a particular experience of dryness in prayer is authentic and God-given when in fact it is something brought on by our own infidelities.

The time of spiritual dryness is a critical time in the spiritual journey. How we respond to it will determine whether we move forward spiritually or make no progress whatsoever.

Question Three: Why does God permit us to experience desert periods in the spiritual journey?

So I will allure her; will lead her into the desert and speak to her heart. (Hosea 2:16)

God permits us to experience spiritual desert periods in order to purify us of those things that hinder our spiritual transformation and to teach us some important lessons about the spiritual life and how it works. Here are some specific purifications that God works in us and lessons that he teaches us in the desert experience of prayer.

There are *purifications* to be borne: In the desert God will want to purify us of any excessive attachment we may have to consolation in prayer. If God blesses us in prayer with a multitude of consolations (or "spiritual highs"), there is a danger that we may seek and love "the consolations of our God more than the God of our consolations" (St. Teresa of Avila). In time of spiritual consolation it is easy to pray. The challenge is to remain faithful to prayer when we experience little or no felt sense of God's presence or action in our lives. During such dry periods God is asking us to love him for himself and not just for the spiritual highs or consolations he offers us in prayer. The Lord is asking us to show that we are not just fair-weather friends but all-weather friends. This kind of purification teaches us that God is to be found more deeply in the desert than in the garden of superficial delights.

At the same time God also wants to purify us of spiritual

vanity. John Dalrymple, in his book *Simple Prayer*, explains spiritual vanity in this way:

> Someone taking to religion in all zeal, becoming caught up in a campaign of prayer, fasting and spiritual reading, liturgical practice, and retreat weekends might be indulging unawares in one big ego-trip. . . . Conversion of the soul from a worldly life to a spiritual life is at first superficial only. The convert has been given new, spiritual goals; but the conversion is only external; in itself the soul is as full as it ever was of unregenerate tendencies to vanity, arrogance, acquisitiveness, the only difference being that after conversion these tendencies are now attached to spiritual instead of worldly objects. . . . The zeal [of such a person] is infectious, but it is, as yet, chiefly the expression of the person's vanity or self-centeredness, dressed up in Christian clothes.

For God to do his work of spiritual transformation in us, he must purify us of such spiritual vanity. God often brings about this purification by bringing to naught our best efforts to change ourselves and everything and everyone around us. As we sit on the ruins of our self-made temples and projects, we are purified of spiritual vanity and arrogance, and we learn the meaning of spiritual poverty: our complete dependence and need for God to bring about any spiritual growth in others or in ourselves.

In the desert God's intention is not to punish us but to purify us. In the journey of life, we consciously or unconsciously become overly attached to persons or objects—so much so that they become idols, and thus more important to us than God. This happened to the Israelites after they lived in the Promised Land for some time. They became so enamored with the blessings of the land that they forgot the One who gave them the land. To purify them of this idolatry, God led the Israelites into the desert for a second time where they would be free of all their attachments and free to listen anew to the Word of God (see Hosea 2:16–25.)

There are also several lessons to be learned: When God takes away consolation in prayer, the first lesson we learn is that God can be encountered at a deeper level than the level of our emotions. God wants to teach us that we are no longer dependent on emotional returns to know we have encountered the Lord. As we grow in our relationship with God, the more we will "learn to be at home in the dark because we are sure, in faith, that the potter is truly shaping the clay, even though the clay sees nothing of what is happening" (Thomas Green, SJ, *When the Well Runs Dry*).

An example about eating food might help to illustrate this point more clearly. Sometimes we may immensely enjoy eating a delicious meal, savoring every morsel of the food. On another occasion we may not enjoy another type of delicious food. We may not be feeling well, or the food may not appeal to us. Yet from the point of view of nutrition, both meals may be equally good. Our lack of enjoyment of the second meal in no way diminishes its nutritional value.

The same principle is at work in prayer life. Sometimes when we pray we really feel and savor God's presence and love. At other times the prayer is empty and dull. Who, then, are we to say that the latter time is of no benefit to our spiritual growth or is less pleasing in God's sight?

A second lesson God teaches us in the desert is that spiritual consolation is God's pure gift to us and not something we can earn by being good or by praying in a particular way. In prayer God teaches this important lesson by "dropping in" on us when we least expect him and by "failing to show" when we very much want to experience his presence.

A third lesson that God wishes to teach us in the desert is that spiritual growth is totally dependent on God's work in us and not on anything we do. Our task is simply to be flexible and cooperative with the movement of the Spirit. In the spiritual life, "working at it" often means "being still," "just being there," and exercising discipline over our doing and achieving self which so often wants to run the show. This is a difficult lesson for us because so much of our training for the journey of life has told us to be self-sufficient and take-charge individuals. It is not easy for us to switch gears in the inner journey.

In the spiritual life God is the Chief Director: We are the individual unique members of the human cast of billions. Mary, at the Annunciation, is our perfect model (see Luke 1:26–38). When God invites her to become the mother of Jesus, she doesn't respond, "Sure, Lord, *I'll* do it!" Rather, she says, "I am your maidservant; work in and through me as you want." Mary's response was, "Be it done unto me," not, "I'll do it." This attitude is one of active receptivity, and it is the secret of Christian spirituality and spiritual growth. Active receptivity is characterized by the effort to place our energy, will, and freedom at the disposal of God so that he can do with us and in us what he wills.

The final lesson that God teaches us when our prayer runs dry is that we must gradually learn to participate in the Cross of Christ. In times of dryness we are experiencing the thirst of Jesus on the Cross. If the Cross was Jesus' way to the Father, then surely we, the disciples of Jesus, cannot expect to travel the scenic route free of all pain and hardship. When we experience darkness in prayer or in the marketplace, we are being invited to identify with Jesus in his suffering and in his experience of feeling abandoned by the Father. Also, in the desert we are being invited and challenged to trust that our God will not abandon us but will come to rescue us and redeem us (see Exodus 16).

Question Four: How can we tell when a particular desert experience is caused by our own infidelity?

If dryness occurs in prayer, particularly in the early stages when God is giving alternating periods of dryness and consolation, we may tend to blame ourselves for our condition. We may wonder what latest infidelity we committed to bring about this dryness. The fact may be that we have done nothing wrong to occasion it. God may be allowing us to experience it because he wants to purify some aspect of our relationship with him or teach us some spiritual lessons—as we have just seen in the last chapter. On the other hand, we may think the dryness is from God when in fact it is caused by our own laxity and sinfulness. Therefore, it is important that we be able to discern its true cause because our response to it will differ, depending on whether the dryness is something permitted by God or something caused by ourselves.

There are various reasons why we may be the cause of our own spiritual dryness. Here are some of them.

First, we may be indifferent to a sinful pattern of behavior. If we are indifferent to some sinful pattern of behavior in our lives, we can expect difficulty in prayer. In a human friendship, a negative pattern of behavior (a critical or lying spirit, for example) that we make no effort to change will have a destructive effect on the whole relationship. Likewise, if in our relationship with God, we are deliberately ignoring a sinful pattern of behavior (for example, involvement in an illicit relationship, unforgiveness, or unethical business practices), we can rightfully expect tension in our relationship with God. When we do something like this, we are deliberately excluding the Lord and his influence from some area of our lives. In such a situation we should not be surprised that we do not feel God's presence in our times of prayer.

Of course it is important to note that this does not refer to a sinful pattern of behavior that we are trying to change and that we are bringing before the Lord in prayer. In this case we are recognizing sin and struggling with it. Instead of keeping us from God, our struggle with a particular sin or weakness may be the very means that God will use to allow us to experience his love, mercy, and power. St. Paul's famous example of how his thorn in the flesh became the very means of God's power is an example of this (see 2 Corinthians 12:7–10).

Second, we may be harboring repressed anger at God. Two highly respected spiritual directors, Frs. William Connolly and William Barry, write in their book, *The Practice of Spiritual Direction*: "When prayer flattens out, or appears to be facing an iron wall, the director must always suspect the presence of unexpressed anger." To add to this problem, many of us were raised in a culture where appropriate expression of anger was socially unacceptable. In this vein, the above authors continue: "Hence resentments, holding a grudge or subdued rage, when they are present, are all likely to be given other names like indifference and rational analysis."

When others hurt us, our relationship with them diminishes. We may try to cover up by presenting an affable, friendly front; but in reality we will distance ourselves emotionally from them. In a similar way, if we become angry with God about something, we may continue to be faithful to our prayer time, but on an emotional level we can be fairly sure we have distanced ourselves from him. It is important for us to realize that if life is handing us a raw deal, we may well be unconsciously blaming God for our unfortunate situation.

Third, dryness may come as a result of our separating prayer from life. The spiritual life is *all* of life and not just one segment of it. The Lord refuses to be a compartmentalized God; he wants to be part and parcel of our whole life. When we try to keep God in church or in our prayer closet and not allow him to guide all the activities of our day, we can be sure that we are setting ourselves up for dryness in prayer. If we exclude God from the activities of our day, we should not be surprised that he is missing from our prayer time. Even on a human level, no one likes to be a "tagalong" in someone else's life.

Fourth, overwork can lead to dryness. When our prayer life dries up, it is good for us to ask if we are pushing ourselves too much on the vital and functional dimensions of life. "Am I overworked? Am I overtired? Am I coming down with the flu? Am I neglecting physical exercise? Do I have a tendency to convert leisure time into work?" These are important questions to ask because their answers affect our prayer life. If we fail to care properly for our bodies, we are neglecting a dimension of ourselves that we depend on to help us to pray. When we are very tired and overworked, prayer may well be seen as just another duty to be performed or something to be done automatically.

Fifth, there may be a lack of honesty in our prayer. Just as shallow or dishonest sharing dulls human relationships, it also dulls the Divine-human relationship. If our prayer is no more than "sweet talk" to "sweet Jesus," we should not expect Jesus to be too interested in our conversation. We must learn to talk to the Lord about the real fabric of our lives.

Sixth, we must avoid halfhearted efforts at prayer. On a human level we may fail to really connect with others because our conversations are just words—words that fail to express what we are truly thinking and feeling. The problem may be that deep down we are scared to encounter each other in a deep way. When a relationship is characterized by this type of communication, we should expect it to be empty and unfulfilling. In a similar vein, when our prayer time consists mainly of the rote recitation of certain prayers or of inattentive spiritual reading—when we merely *say* prayers and *perform* acts of piety with no real desire to encounter God and grow in relationship with the Lord—we should expect little or no satisfaction in prayer. In fact, our spiritual exercises may become a substitute for a real relationship with God.

If we discern that we are the cause of our spiritual dryness, we should do all we can to remove the particular obstacle. For example, if the problem is that we are holding onto a grudge and doing nothing to let it go, we may need to pray the prayer of forgiveness suggested in chapter five, or we may need to speak openly to the person with whom we are having a problem. If we discern that our experience of spiritual dryness is due to our tendency to separate prayer from life, our solution will be to work at allowing the Lord to walk with us in all the activities of our day.

In short, when we discern that we ourselves are the cause of the spiritual dryness, we ought to do something to remove the obstacle. Judging from the experience of most, if not all, disciples of the Lord, once we begin to struggle with an obstacle, prayer again becomes alive and we experience a new closeness to God. Of course, in trying to discern the cause of our spiritual dryness, it would be well to seek the counsel of a good spiritual director. Most of us tend to think that spiritual dryness is due to some infidelity on our part. The truth may be that God is permitting us to experience the desert so he can continue his purifying work in us—which leads us directly to the next question.

Question Five: What indications do we have that God might be permitting our spiritual dryness to continue his purifying work within us?

While we can never be absolutely sure—since we live by faith and not by clear vision—when spiritual dryness is being permitted by God, we can say that the following are good indications that the dryness is the purifying work of God:

- If during the time of dryness we remain faithful to prayer

- If our prayer is honest and flows from the real fabric of our lives

- If we are trying to integrate prayer and life

- If we are trying to live a life of charity; if our prayer helps us to be more loving

- If we are genuinely trying to avoid sin and live our lives according to God's Word

- If we thirst for God as we walk in the desert

It is crucial to remember that our desire for God is in itself a tangible sign of his presence in our lives. We couldn't even desire God if he didn't place that desire in our hearts.

Prayer, like so many other aspects of life, is a series of "arrivals" and "starting points." We arrive at a point where we feel good. We experience the grace of consolation. But that lasts only a little while and then a certain discontent (a kind of desert) sets in—a discontent that may be caused by ourselves or permitted by God. Then we are faced with the challenge of discerning who is causing the discontent: "Is it God or me?" The purpose of the discontent caused by God is to create in us a longing for more, to create in us a desire to move closer to the Lord. In the spiritual journey God brings us to a particular point or state; he lets us rest there and enjoy that plateau for a little while, and then he says, "Okay. Let's move ahead and seek for more" (see Exodus 40:36–37). Of course, it is not easy to move when we are not sure where he is leading us. All he says is, "Move, and trust that I'll take you to a new and better place." If our thoughts, words, or actions are the cause of dryness and discontent, it is necessary for us—with God's guidance—to chart a new course for our spiritual life.

In summary, if we are in doubt about the cause of our discontent or dryness, we should talk to a spiritual guide or, if that is not possible, simply say a prayer like this: "Lord, if this dryness I am experiencing is due to some failing of mine, please reveal it to me. Until you do, I am going to assume that I am not the cause of the dryness."

Question Six: What are some measures we can take to help sustain us in our spiritual dryness?

There are four measures available.

First, we should find a wise spiritual director. A wise spiritual director is one who understands the role of the desert in the spiritual life and hopefully one who has experienced and grown through the desert experience in his or her own spiritual journey. Many people whom God led into the desert for purification have suffered much at the hands of well-intentioned but misinformed spiritual guides. (St. John of the Cross reserves some of his harshest words for this type of spiritual director.) A misinformed guide, for example, may insist that we continue to meditate and double our spiritual reading when God is actually calling us to the prayer of contemplation.

A good desert-experienced spiritual director will always be a source of guidance, encouragement, and inspiration. That is why—when we are spiritually dry—it is so important that we find and place our trust in a good and wise director. But, as most of us know, wise spiritual directors are nearly as scarce as palm trees in Alaska. The truth is that the road to authenticity is dangerous, hard, and narrow, and few decide to travel it. In the absence of a wise spiritual director (and there is really no substitute for such a person), we may receive some guidance from books that are written or recommended by people who are recognized guides of the inner journey.

Second, we need to maintain a strong faith. This will enable us to believe that:

God knows what he is doing when he allows us to experience the desert (see Romans 11:33–36);

In the desert God is not punishing us but is purifying us (see Deuteronomy 30:6);

God grows his best flowers (virtues) in the desert (see Hosea 2:1–11);

God works in us while we rest in him (see Mark 4:26–29);

In the struggles of life God is on our side fighting our battles (see Exodus 14:13-14 and Deuteronomy 1:30-33);

In the desert God's seeming absence is just a different type of presence, one that we may not as yet have recognized (see Exodus 16);

We can be secure with insecurity (see Romans 8:28);

We should abandon ourselves generously to the purifying work of God (see Luke 23:46).

Third, we should remain faithful to prayer. In the desert, prayer is usually dry, and therefore we find it difficult to remain faithful to it. For this reason, spiritual guides counsel us to avoid two extremes or temptations. The first temptation is to quit prayer, thinking that our best efforts are leading us nowhere. The second is to overload our prayer time with extra prayers, rosaries, Scripture reading, and more. It is not helpful to think that if we try harder, we will once more feel the presence of God. This second temptation needs to be resisted not only because it blocks God's purpose in the desert, but also because it is (usually unconsciously) our attempt to remain active and in control of the prayer process.

In general, prayer in the desert leads us to be much less active and much more passive—less us, more God. The desert challenge involves learning to sit quietly in the presence of God, trusting that he is at work in us while we rest in him. Learning to "waste time and do nothing" in prayer is, without a doubt, one of the most difficult lessons we have to learn in the school of prayer. Unfortunately most of us never learn to waste time gracefully in the presence of God. Such a practice goes completely against our Western, work-ethic nature—a nature that drives us to do, to achieve, and to produce. We are conditioned not to be satisfied until we see tangible results for our efforts. Because of this need, most of us fill the vacuum that we feel in the desert with reading or prayers of some sort. For those of us who are willing to try to do less (that is, to be less active) in prayer so that God may do more in us, the following suggestions might be helpful.

Spend some time just being present with the Lord, aware that as we rest in him he is at work in us. Put aside all effort to achieve "success" in prayer and realize that achievement (growth) is God's work.

Spend some time slowly repeating prayers such as: "Incline my heart according to your will, O Lord" and "Make me want you, O Lord, more than anyone/anything in my life."

Take a phrase of Scripture such as, "You are my beloved Son," and dwell on it.

Take one word like "Jesus" or "love" and repeat it gently and slowly, letting God do the work, leading us beyond conceptual thoughts, images, or feelings to wordless depths.

Be present with Mary after she lost Jesus (see Luke 2:41–50) and at the foot of the cross (see John 19:25–27), which must have been a real dark night of the spirit for her. Then ask Mary to intercede for us so that we may have something of the faith which she had when she thought she had lost Jesus.

Read up on spiritual dryness. Reading and rereading portions of a book like Thomas Green's *When the Well Runs Dry* will encourage us to persevere in the desert.

When we pray we must place ourselves at God's disposal. What actually happens at prayer is God's business. This piece of wisdom should help to free us from thinking that it is up to us to make things happen in prayer. Once we relax, knowing that our role is to be faithful in coming aside, we can eliminate distractions from within and without and pray as we feel led. ("Pray as you can, not as you can't.") The rest is in God's hands. If God chooses to bless us with a deep sense of his presence, we should indeed be very grateful. If the Lord chooses to bless us with his *seeming* absence (God is always only *seemingly* absent), we should try to be grateful for that—because we believe that God knows what will best help us to grow. According to Fr. John Dalrymple, "Our prayer is good when our hearts are fixed on God, even if it is filled with boring aridity or passionate turmoil."

Fourth, we should seek the support of fellow pilgrims. While each person's inner journey is very personal and unique, much can be learned from the journeys of co-pilgrims. Only the foolish try to travel the inner journey alone. In the desert we are all beggars sharing morsels of bread with each other. Also, if we are blessed enough to be part of a small, faith-sharing group, we have available to us an excellent resource for the dry times. In the dry times the prayers of fellow pilgrims are usually a big help.

Finally, this prayer of Henri Nouwen, taken from his book, *A Cry for Mercy: Prayers from the Genesee*, can be a source of great encouragement during times of spiritual dryness and desolation:

Dear Lord, in the midst of much inner turmoil and restlessness, there is a consoling thought: maybe you are working in me in a way I cannot yet feel, experience or understand. My mind is not able to concentrate on you, my heart is not able to remain centered, and it seems as if you are absent and have left me alone. But in faith I cling to you. I believe that your Spirit reaches deeper and further than my mind or heart, and that profound movements are not the first to be noticed.

Therefore, Lord, I promise I will not run away, not give up, not stop praying, even when it all seems useless, pointless, and a waste of time and effort. I want to let you know that I love you even though I do not feel loved by you, and that I hope in you even though I often experience despair. Let this be a little dying I can do with you and for you as a way of experiencing some solidarity with the millions in this world who suffer far more than I do. Amen.

Questions for Personal Reflection and Small-Group Discussion

1. What spoke to you most in this chapter?
2. What has been your experience with spiritual dryness in the past?
3. Has this chapter helped you discover some possible reasons why you suffer spiritual dryness at times?
4. Which of the six lessons mentioned in this chapter helps you the most?
5. What was your experience with the suggested prayer exercise offered below?

Suggested Prayer Exercise

Reflect on some dry periods (or a dry period) in your life. Looking back, can you see any good that came from it? What seemed to be the dominant feeling you had during the dry period: anger, frustration, discouragement, confusion, or anxiety? Were you able to talk to the Lord about such feelings?

Conclusion

God very much desires each of us to come to the point where we look forward to spending time with him and feeling at ease in his presence. God doesn't want us to be constantly anxious and insecure about our relationship with him, and he does not want us to see prayer (our time with God) as something we think we must do if we are to make it to heaven. Who of us would like to have a friend who relates to us only because he or she feels some obligation to do so? Yet, too often, isn't that the way we see our relationship with God? Frequently addressing God in prayer is treated as another obligation to which we have to attend.

When we come to the point of praying because we want to spend time with God, we have been given a great grace. It is a grace that all of us should pray for on a regular basis. We could pray that we can make our own the longing for God of which the psalmist wrote:

> O God, you are my God whom I seek; for you my flesh pines and my soul thirsts like the earth, parched, lifeless and without water. (Psalm 63:2)

If we normally want to spend time with God, the way to go about it will be relatively simple. In our human friendships, two very important questions need to be asked: "Do the persons seeking to relate really want to be with each other? Do they normally like each other?" If they do not want to be to-gether and do not like each other, their best efforts to relate will fail. On the other hand, if they sincerely like each other's company and are committed to being friends, it will be easy enough for them to find ways, times, and places to be together. They may do this in various ways: going for a walk, attending a movie, eating out together, or just sitting at home together. They may contact each other early in the morning or late at night. At times their contact with each other may be either a quick "hello" on the phone or a long, in-depth conversation. Sometimes one party may do nearly all the talking while the other listens patiently.

As it is with our friends, so it is, or should be, between God and us. If God is someone we truly want to befriend, we will not have a big problem discovering ways, times, and places to express our relationship with the Lord.

We can spend time with God in countless ways: talking, listening to the Word, praising, thanking, repenting, peti-tioning, complaining, weeping, seeking guidance, waiting for revelation, admiring creation, praying the Rosary, singing, dancing, reading, or just resting in the Lord's presence. The main point is that we are sincerely trying to be there for and with the Lord. The central idea is wanting to be with God and wanting to be sensitive and responsive to the Lord's prompt-ings; the rest is secondary.

We should feel free to reach out to God at any time and in any place. At times our contact with him will be like a brief phone call during which we say: "Hi, love you," or "Help! I 'goofed'; please forgive me," or "Wow, what a sunrise this morning; it was great!"

There will be times when our conversations are more in-depth: We'll talk about serious personal problems, or we'll take extra time to do spiritual reading, journaling, or contemplation. The important point is that we don't leave our contact with God to chance. It is good to pray when we feel like it. But if we pray only when we feel like it, there is a real chance that God may get the leftover scraps of our day. No one likes to get the leftover scraps of another person's day, especially when that person is considered to be a friend.

If we look to God as a friend, we will make sure that time with him is part of our daily schedule and not something left to chance. We will be certain that our contact with God is more than the quick phone calls that are made as we run from one engagement to another. Of course, some people's circumstances in life will leave them with much more time to pray. God understands each of our situations and is willing to work within our limitations.

To repeat, the important point is wanting to spend time with God and proving that by frequently connecting with him as we move through the day. The how, where, and when of our prayer is a secondary issue. What really matters is that we have a heart that truly seeks him. "Yes, when you seek me with all your heart, you will find me with you . . ." (Jeremiah 29:13–14). What matters is that we have a heart that seeks to be filled with God's love and seeks to be a channel of that love to all of creation.

How to Use This Book for Small-Group Discussion

When they entered the city they went to the
upper room where they were staying, Peter
and John and James and Andrew, Philip and
Thomas, Bartholomew and Matthew, James son
of Alphaeus, Simon the Zealot, and Judas son
of James. All these devoted themselves with one
accord to prayer, together with some women, and
Mary the mother of Jesus, and his brothers.

ACTS 1:13–14

Joining fully with sisters and brothers in
worship . . . neutralizes a tendency toward
excessive self-centeredness and fosters a spirit of
charity, of love reaching out toward others.

JOSEPH M. CHAMPLIN

A small-group discussion of a book invariably leads to a deeper understanding and appreciation of the contents. In sharing our reflections on the contents of a book, we can point out to each other details we would otherwise have missed. The actual verbalization of our responses to the questions at the end of each chapter and our listening to the other participants' reflections will lead to a greater clarity and depth of understanding of the subject matter.

When we participate in a small-group discussion of a book, we often receive helpful insights and personal experiences related to the topic. In short, the shared reflections of several people who have read a book together usually provide a much richer experience than just a private reading of the material.

Some Things to Decide

Before starting, the small group will need to decide on the following:

- This book has seventeen chapters. How many weeks does the group want to spend studying the book?
    - seventeen weeks—i.e., one week for each chapter?
    - eight weeks—i.e., two chapters each meeting?
    - six weeks—and decide what chapters to focus on during that period?
- How long will the meetings last?
- Where will the meetings take place?

- What format will be used use?
- Will there be refreshments and fellowship at the end of the meetings?

SUGGESTED FORMAT

Opening Prayer

Participants could take turns saying the opening prayer each week. If helpful, the group could also pray together the following prayer:

> *Father, we thank you for gathering us together for this time of sharing and reflection. Open our hearts to your Holy Spirit who is present and active in each of us. Help us to share our thoughts, feelings, and experiences. Help us also to listen to one another with love and respect. Bind us together in love and help us to be clear channels of your wisdom and love for one another. This we ask through Christ our Lord. Amen.*

If the participants do not know each other, consider spending some time becoming acquainted. The following format may be helpful.

Ask each participant to share their name, home state, length of time in the parish, favorite pastime, and their motivation to join the group.

At the first meeting, if some of the participants have not

read a chapter, consider reading the opening chapter, "What Is Prayer?" They could rotate reading the various paragraphs. [Since some people do not like to read in public, the facilitator could say: "If you do not like to read in public, just say 'pass' when your turn comes."]

If the participants decide to read chapter one at the first meeting, they can share the questions provided at the end of the chapter. Because any small group will likely have people who are always ready to share as well as a few who are reluctant to share, it may be helpful for the facilitator to say the following before the sharing begins:

In order to give everyone a chance to share, we will go around the room and invite all of you to share your response to the first question which is: What spoke to you most in the chapter? If you are not ready to share, just say "pass." When a person shares, you may feel like commenting on what was said. I ask that you refrain from doing so until everyone has had a chance to share. To help get this step started, I will begin and then move to my left.

After the round is completed, the facilitator could say something like: "Thank you for sharing what spoke to you most in the chapter. I am wondering if anyone has a comment on what you have just heard." Then pause for at least fifteen seconds.

At this point the facilitator will need to decide if he/she wants to go around the room again or just open up the discussion and see who responds to the second question. The same applies to questions three and four. If the facilitator observes that only a few people have responded to questions two, three, and four, perhaps he or she may decide to mix it up a bit by going around the room on questions one and three. In this way, all present will have an opportunity to respond to two of the four questions. This is also a great way to have some control over the talkers in the group. Small group facilitators should also feel free to create their own questions, especially if the questions at the end of each chapter are not evoking much response.

CONSIDER THE MESSAGE

After spending an hour and a half to two hours discussing a particular chapter and sharing personal experiences, it would be a good idea to give the group a minute of silence to consider what message they are taking away with them. The facilitator could introduce this section of the session with these words:

> We have had a lot of wonderful sharing today. At this time, I invite you to pause for a minute to give each of you a chance to think about what message you are taking away with you today/this evening. If you feel free to share the message after the silent pause, that would be great. But first, let's take a minute to ponder on what spoke to us most today.

The facilitator should not be afraid to have a full minute of silence. If someone jumps in after ten seconds, gently say: "_____, would you hold your thought for a moment?" This fosters discipline and helps the participants become comfortable with silent pauses.

CONCLUDE WITH PRAYERS OF PETITION, INTERCESSION, AND THANKSGIVING

The facilitator can introduce this concluding part of the meeting with these or similar words:

> I suggest we conclude our time together with prayers of petition, intercession and thanksgiving. Perhaps you have some special intentions you would like for the group to pray for, prayers relevant to today's subject, prayers for things going on in our larger world, and maybe prayers of thanksgiving for blessings in your life.

The facilitator should suggest to participants to address their prayers of petition, intercession, and thanksgiving directly to God (e.g., "Lord, I lift up to you my spouse who is ill") rather than simply telling the group what it is they would like prayers for (e.g., "I would like prayers for my spouse"). The desire becomes a prayer when it is directly addressed to God.

ROLE OF THE GROUP FACILITATOR

The role of the facilitator is to keep the participants focused on the topic being discussed. The facilitator also prevents any one or two people from dominating the exchange by encouraging all participants to share both their thoughts and their personal experiences.

In the initial stages of a small-group experience, especially when the participants do not know one another, there may be a tendency for the facilitator to consciously, but more often unconsciously, take on the role of "answer-person" or "group expert." The participants themselves may unconsciously place the group leader in that role. It is crucial for the group leader not to allow himself or herself to become the "answer person" or "dominant talker." This is particularly important in a discussion of a book on prayer when everyone will have insights and experiences to share. No one individual should present himself or herself as expert or teacher of the rest. If people are looking for lectures or mini-sermons on prayer, most likely they will go somewhere other than a small group to meet that need.

If facilitators find that the participants have a tendency to look to them for all the answers, they can deal with this potential problem by simply asking, "Can anyone help (name of participant) with that question?"

It should also be noted that the role of the facilitator occasionally involves helping the participants evaluate their small-group experience in the course of a meeting. This evaluation can be done by asking the participants to respond to the following questions:

- What has been helpful or good about our shared experience thus far?
- What has not been helpful or what has been frustrating or hindering the process?
- Is there anything we can do to enrich the group experience?

The facilitator may need to encourage the participants to be honest in their evaluation of how the process is working. In one-to-one or group relationships, "being nice" and saying only what people want to hear may facilitate harmony, but it will also bring on stagnation. On the other hand, giving constructive criticism may be a risk; but where there is openness, this invariably brings about growth and improvement in the group process.

HOW TO BE A GOOD PARTICIPANT

The degree of openness and participation by the members of a small group will determine to a great extent the quality of the experience for all the participants.

Participants will enrich a small-group process by:
- reading beforehand the assigned pages for each meeting in a prayerful and reflective manner

- sharing their thoughts, feelings, or personal experiences of the subject matter
- actively listening when other participants share their reflections
- encouraging and affirming participants who tend to hesitate to share trying to keep the group focused on the topic
- offering an honest evaluation of the group process when invited to do so
- praying for the spiritual success and growth of the group

Participants will hinder and obstruct the small-group process by:

- failing to prepare the assignment for each meeting
- complaining and using the small-group discussion to air their pet peeves
- rambling and talking off the topic
- harshly criticizing the reflections of others
- dominating the discussion by acting as if they have a monopoly on the Holy Spirit
- offering only heady remarks and rarely, if ever, sharing a personal experience
- never participating in the sharing process

It would be wise for the facilitator to have the participants reflect on these characteristics of helpful and unhelpful participants after the opening prayer of the first session. It might also be helpful to review this section after a few sessions, particularly if the facilitator thinks some of the group seem to show evidence of being unhelpful participants.

If you have any questions about the use of this book in a small-group setting, feel free to email me at tobin2@live.com.

About the Author

Father Eamon Tobin, a native of Kilkenny, Ireland, obtained his master's degree in Formative Spirituality from Duquesne University, Pittsburgh, Pennsylvania. Fr. Tobin is currently pastor of Ascension Catholic Church, Melbourne, Florida. Visit his parish website, www.ascensioncatholic.net, for his writings on the *Catechism*, the Sunday readings, Church history, and more. He is the author of the book *How to Forgive Yourself & Others.*

Bibliography

Alphonsus Liguori, Saint. *To Love Christ Jesus*. Edited by Nancy Fearon, and Christopher Farrell, C.SS.R. Liguori, MO: Liguori Publications, 1987.

Anonymous. *The Cloud of Unknowing*. Translated by William Johnson, S.J. Garden City, NY: Doubleday, 1973.

Barry, William, S.J. *God and You*. Mahwah, NJ: Paulist Press, 1988.

Champlin, Joseph M. *Behind Closed Doors*. Mahwah, NJ: Paulist Press, 1984.

Connolly, William, and William Barry. *The Practice of Spiritual Direction*. New York, NY: Harper and Row, 1982.

Dalrymple, John. *Letting Go in Love*. Wilmington, DE: Michael Glazier, Inc., 1987.

   Simple Prayer. Wilmington, DE: Michael Glazier, Inc., 1984.

de Caussade, Jean-Pierre. *Abandonment to Divine Providence*. Garden City, NY: Doubleday, 1975.

Documents of Vatican II, Walter M. Abbott, S.J., General Editor. New York, NY: Guild Press, 1966.

Dyckman, Katherine Marie, S.N.J.M., and L. Patrick Carroll, S.J. *Solitude to Sacrament*. Collegeville, MN: The Liturgical Press, 1982.

Finley, Mitch. "Recovering the Rosary." *America*. May 7, 1983.

Fischer, Ed. "The Recorded Life." *Notre Dame Magazine*. December, 1981.

Grace, John Patrick. *Hearing His Voice*. Notre Dame, IN: Ave Maria Press, 1979.

Greeley, Andrew. *The Bottom-Line Catechism for Contemporary Catholics*. Chicago, IL: The Thomas More Press, 1982.

Green, Thomas H. *Opening to God*. Notre Dame, IN: Ave Maria Press, 1977.

Weeds Among the Wheat. Notre Dame, IN: Ave Maria Press, 1984.

When the Well Runs Dry. Notre Dame, IN: Ave Maria Press, 1979.

Guigo II. *The Ladder of Monks and Twelve Meditations.* Translated by Edmund Colledge and James Walsh. Kalamazoo, MI: Cistercian Publishing Company, 1981.

Hauser, Richard, S.J. *In His Spirit: A Guide to Today's Spirituality.* Mahwah, NJ: Paulist Press, 1982.

Moving in the Spirit. Mahwah, NJ: Paulist Press, 1986.

Hofinger, Johannes, S.J. *Pastoral Life in the Power of the Spirit.* New York, NY: Alba House, 1982.

Hughes, Gerard. *God of Surprises.* Mahwah, NJ: Paulist Press, 1986.

John of the Cross, St. *The Collected Works of Saint John of the Cross.* Translated by Kieran Kavanaugh, O.C.D., and Otilio Rodriguez. Washington, DC: I.C.S. Publications, 1979.

Kelsey, Morton T. *The Adventure Inward.* Minneapolis, MN: Augsburg Publishing House.

The Other Side of Silence. Mahwah, NJ: Paulist Press, 1976.

Linn, Matthew, S.J., Dennis Linn, S.J., and Sheila Fabricant. *Prayer Course in Healing Life's Hurts.* Mahwah, NJ: Paulist Press, 1983.

McManus, Jim, C.SS.R. *The Healing Power of the Sacraments.* Notre Dame, IN: Ave Maria Press, 1984.

McNamara, William, O.C.D. *The Human Adventure.* Warwick, NY: Amity House, 1988.

Muto, Susan A. *A Practical Guide to Spiritual Reading.* Denville, NJ: Dimension Books, 1976.

Pathways of Spiritual Living. Petersham, MA: St. Bede's Publications, 1988.

Nouwen, Henri J. M. *A Cry for Mercy: Prayers from the Genesee.* Garden City, NY: Image Books, A Division of Doubleday, 1983.

Pearse, Padraic. *Plays, Stories, Poems.* Dublin: Helican Press, 1980.

Pennington, Basil, O.C.S.O. *Centering Prayer: Renewing an Ancient Christian Prayer Form.* Garden City, NY: Doubleday, 1982.

Finding Grace at the Center. Edited by Thomas Keating. Petersham, MA: St. Bede's Publications, 1979.

Ways of Prayer. Wilmington, DE: Michael Glazier, Inc., 1982.

Pennock, Michael F. *The Ways of Prayer: An Introduction.* Notre Dame, IN: Ave Maria Press, 1987.

Pilkington, Evan. *Learning to Pray.* London: Darton, Longman & Todd, Ltd., 1986.

Pollard, Miriam, O.C.S.O. *The Laughter of God: At Ease with Prayer.* Wilmington, DE: Michael Glazier, Inc., 1986.

Powell, John, S.J. *The Christian Vision: The Truth That Sets Us Free.* Valencia, CA: Tabor Publications, 1984.

Rosage, David E. *Discovering Pathways to Prayer.* Locust Valley, NY: Living Flame Press, 1975.

The Sacramental Path to Peace. Locust Valley, NY: Living Flame Press, 1984.

Shannon, William. *Seeking the Face of God.* New York, NY: Crossroads Publishing Company, 1988.

Shea, John. Article in *U.S. Catholic.* March, 1979.

Tobin, Eamon. *How to Forgive Yourself and Others: Steps to Reconciliation.* Liguori, MO: Liguori Publications, 1983.

United States Catholic Conference. *Behold Your Mother: Woman of Faith.* Washington, DC: United States Catholic Conference, 1973.

Spiritual Renewal of the American Priesthood. Washington, DC: United States Catholic Conference, 1973.

van Breemen, Peter G. *Certain as the Dawn.* Denville, NJ: Dimension Books, 1980.

Whalen, William. "How Catholic Prayer Became a Mass Movement." *U.S. Catholic.* September, 1983.

Wolff, Pierre. *May I Hate God?* Mahwah, NJ: Paulist Press, 1979.

Rediscover Jesus
Matthew Kelly

HAVE YOU EVER WONDERED HOW THE CATHOLIC FAITH COULD HELP YOU LIVE BETTER?

How it could help you find more *joy* at work, *manage* your personal finances, *improve* your marriage, or make you a *better* parent?

THERE IS GENIUS IN CATHOLICISM.

When *Catholicism* is lived as it is intended to be, it elevates every part of our lives. It may sound simple, but they say *genius is taking something complex and making it simple.*

Dynamic Catholic started with a dream: to help ordinary people discover the *genius of Catholicism.*

Wherever you are in your journey, we want to meet you there and walk with you, *step by step,* helping you to discover God and become *the-best-version-of-yourself.*

**To find more helpful resources, visit us
online at DynamicCatholic.com.**

■ Dynamic Catholic

FEED YOUR SOUL.